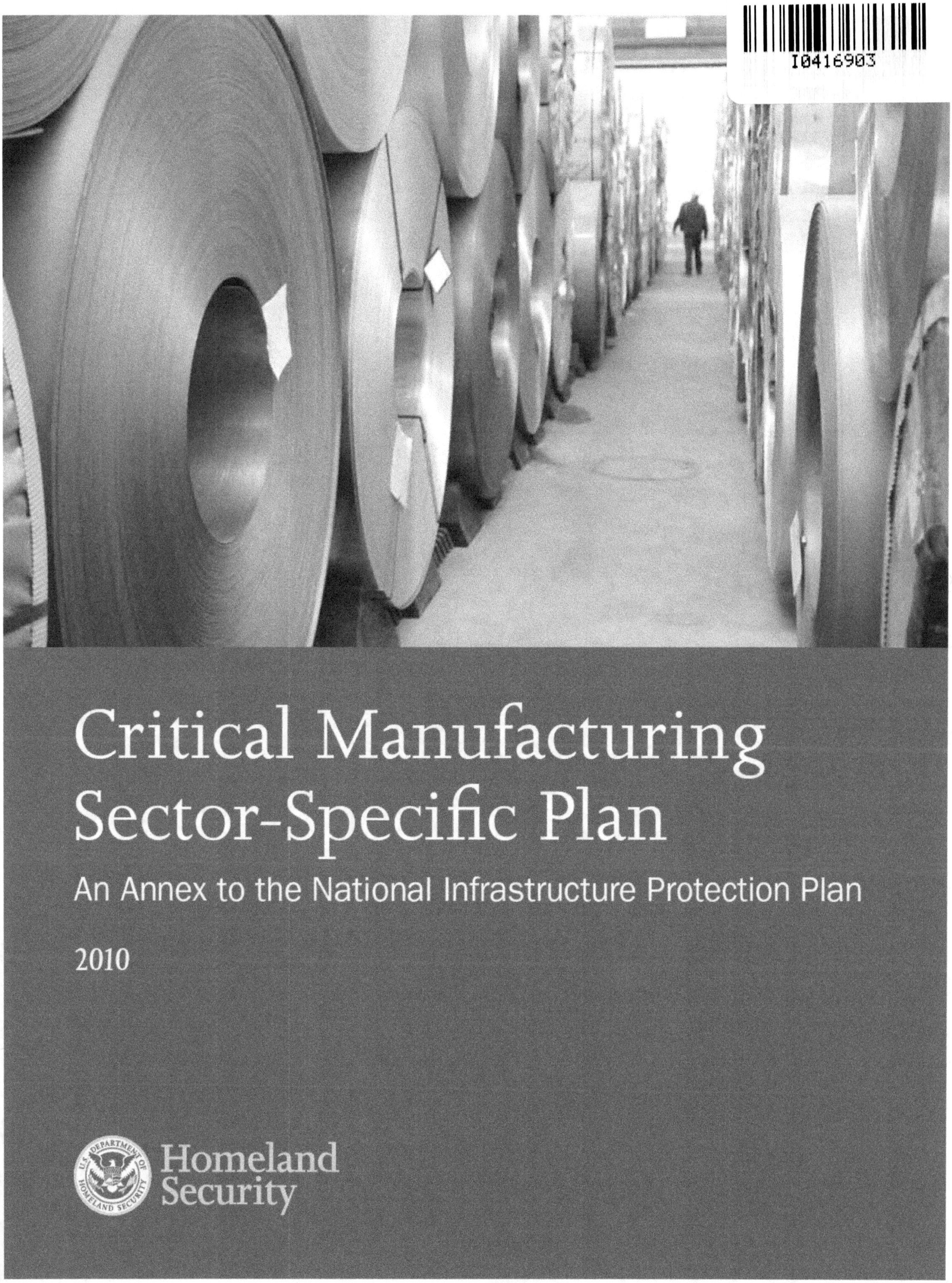

Critical Manufacturing Sector-Specific Plan

An Annex to the National Infrastructure Protection Plan

2010

Homeland Security

Preface

The Critical Manufacturing Sector is crucial to the economic continuity and prosperity of the United States. The U.S. manufacturing industry contributes greatly to the gross domestic product and employs roughly one million members of the Nation's workforce. While the contributions of the sector to the Nation are immense, they do not come without risk; the economic and strategic value of the industry may make it an attractive target for terrorists. Additionally, the economic and strategic value of the industry and existing interdependencies with other sectors may result in significant consequences in the event of a natural disaster or other incident that affects the Critical Manufacturing Sector. To help manage this risk, the U.S. Department of Homeland Security (DHS) and other Critical Manufacturing Sector partners have developed the Critical Manufacturing Sector-Specific Plan (SSP).

The Critical Manufacturing Sector was established by DHS in 2008; this document represents the original Critical Manufacturing SSP. The SSP provides the unifying structure for the integration of sector protection efforts into a single national program to help achieve the goal of safer, more resilient infrastructure. As an annex to the National Infrastructure Protection Plan (NIPP), the Critical Manufacturing SSP describes how the NIPP risk management framework—the six-step process for managing the risks associated with protecting the Nation's critical infrastructure and key resources (CIKR)—is being implemented and integrated with voluntary programs already underway in the sector.

Examples of Critical Manufacturing Sector accomplishments since the sector was established in 2008 include:

- Establishing the Critical Manufacturing Sector-Specific Agency (SSA), Sector Coordinating Council, and Government Coordinating Council to facilitate proper management and oversight of the sector and ensure public-private participation in Critical Manufacturing Sector protection and resilience activities.

- Participating in the National Critical Infrastructure Prioritization Program, to identify an initial list of the most significant assets, systems, and networks.

- Working with sector partners to define sector goals and objectives and develop the Critical Manufacturing SSP.

- Collaborating with the Defense Industrial Base Sector to assess risks posed to certain manufacturing facilities.

- Performing SSA site visits and participating in Enhanced Critical Infrastructure Protection visits to Critical Manufacturing facilities.

- Sponsoring security clearances for Critical Manufacturing Sector members.

- Developing the Homeland Security Information Network Critical Manufacturing site, enabling robust, two-way information sharing among government and industry partners in the sector.

Each year, the Critical Manufacturing Sector CIKR Protection Annual Report will provide updates on the sector's efforts to identify, prioritize, and coordinate the protection of its critical infrastructure. The Sector Annual Report provides the current priorities of the sector as well as the progress made during the past year in implementing the programs and strategies set out in the Critical Manufacturing SSP.

This SSP represents a collaborative effort between the private sector; State, local, tribal, and territorial governments; nongovernmental organizations; and the Federal Government. This collaboration and the approach outlined in this document will result in the prioritization of protection and resilience initiatives and investments within the sector to ensure that resources are applied where they contribute the most to risk mitigation by reducing vulnerabilities, deterring threats, and minimizing the consequences of attacks and other incidents.

The Critical Manufacturing Sector Coordinating Council and Government Coordinating Council are pleased to support this Critical Manufacturing SSP and look forward to a continued partnership with DHS to sustain and enhance the protection and resilience of the Critical Manufacturing Sector.

Todd M. Keil

Assistant Secretary for
Infrastructure Protection
U.S. Department of Homeland Security

W. Craig Conklin

Director
SSA Executive Management Office
U.S. Department of Homeland Security
Chair, Critical Manufacturing GCC

Michael A. Bruggeman

Chair
Critical Manufacturing
Sector Coordinating Council

Table of Contents

List of Figures

List of Tables

Executive Summary

The Critical Manufacturing Sector is an integral component of the U.S. economy, contributing greatly to the US gross domestic product and employing roughly one million of the Nation's workforce. While the contributions the Critical Manufacturing Sector makes to the Nation are immense, they do not come without risk; the economic and strategic value of the industry may make it an attractive target for terrorists. Additionally, the economic and strategic value of the industry may result in significant consequences in the event of a natural disaster or other incident that affects the Critical Manufacturing Sector. To help manage this risk, the Department of Homeland Security (DHS) and other Critical Manufacturing partners have developed the Critical Manufacturing Sector-Specific Plan (SSP).

The SSP provides the unifying structure for the integration of Critical Manufacturing Sector protection efforts into a single national program to help achieve the goal of a safer, more resilient infrastructure. An annex to the National Infrastructure Protection Plan (NIPP), the SSP describes how the NIPP risk management framework—the six-step process for managing the risks associated with protecting the Nation's critical infrastructure and key resources (CIKR)—is being implemented and integrated with voluntary programs already underway in the Critical Manufacturing Sector.

1. Sector Profile and Goals

The Critical Manufacturing Sector is extremely diverse and encompasses several different functional activities, each of which produces a variety of products and materials. By examining the value chain and the services that support it, Critical Manufacturing Sector infrastructure can be divided based on four key functional areas: (1) Primary Metals Manufacturing, (2) Machinery Manufacturing, (3) Electrical Equipment Manufacturing, and (4) Transportation and Heavy Equipment Manufacturing. Each of these key functional areas depends upon physical, cyber, and human elements to perform their missions. Physical elements include the facilities that support each functional area. Human elements include the personnel associated with each of the functions. Finally, cyber elements include electronic systems for processing the information necessary for management and operation or for automatic control of physical processes.

Many Critical Manufacturing assets, systems, and networks are dependent on elements of other CIKR sector assets, systems, and networks to maintain functionality. In some cases, a failure in one sector will have a significant impact on the ability of another sector to perform necessary functions. It is extremely important to identify dependencies and interdependencies at asset, system, and network levels. Careful identification of dependencies and interdependencies is critical to understanding the consequences of a successful attack or natural disaster on infrastructure and identifying the manner in which incidents affecting other infrastructure could impact an interdependent asset, system, network, or function.

Sector Partners. In each CIKR sector, a variety of different entities play roles in ensuring the protection and resiliency of the sector, including all levels of government and the private sector. These entities often are referred to as "sector partners." In the

Critical Manufacturing Sector, the primary Federal sector partners are represented on the Critical Manufacturing Government Coordinating Council (CMGCC), which is chaired by DHS.

The private sector also is a key sector partner, including Critical Manufacturing facility owners and operators. The primary means of government interaction with the private sector comes through the Critical Manufacturing Sector Coordinating Council (CMSCC). The CMSCC includes private sector manufacturing companies and firms of any size that comprise U.S. critical infrastructure and/or provide key resources, or that are considered iconic representatives of the U.S. economy.

Many State, local, tribal, and territorial government entities also play a valuable role in sector CIKR protection. The Sector-Specific Agency (SSA), coordinating with the State, Local, Tribal, and Territorial Government Coordinating Council (SLTTGCC) as well as other avenues, works closely with these partners. The sector is also working to identify international partners who have a role in helping secure or enhance resiliency in the Critical Manufacturing Sector.

Sector Goals. In the Critical Manufacturing SSP, the sector enumerates its mission, goals, and objectives for Critical Manufacturing Sector CIKR protection. These items reflect the overall risk management outcomes that the Critical Manufacturing SSA, SCC, and GCC seek to produce.

Mission Statement for the Critical Manufacturing Sector

Reduce risks to the Critical Manufacturing Sector through proactive prevention, preparation for and mitigation of natural and man-made threats leading to effective response and recovery through public-private partnership.

---

2. Identify Assets, Systems, and Networks

Effective management of Critical Manufacturing Sector protective efforts using a risk-based approach requires identifying what infrastructure (i.e., assets, systems and networks) comprise the sector. To keep identification efforts at a more manageable level, the sector must establish criteria, metrics, and/or thresholds to help identify significant assets, systems, and networks and to identify information requirements that will aid in focusing information collection efforts. As a primary method of gathering information on the assets, systems, and networks of the Critical Manufacturing Sector, DHS will continue to leverage previously initiated data-collection efforts, including continued coordination with Federal, State, and local entities. DHS will work with the CMSCC and CMGCC both to review current methods of data collection and to identify and discuss other potential means for data collection that may be more efficient or encompassing, or less expensive, than current data-collection methods.

DHS utilizes a distributed IT architecture to integrate existing data sets from Federal, State, and commercial sources into a virtual federated database, the Infrastructure Data Warehouse (IDW). This architecture allows numerous CIKR partners to maintain and verify data on sector infrastructure, reduces duplication of effort, distributes information management, and provides access to a more robust and complete data set that retrieves information from multiple noncontiguous databases.

3. Assess Risks (Consequences, Vulnerabilities, and Threats)

The cornerstone of both the NIPP and the SSPs is the NIPP risk management framework (see figure ES-1) that establishes the processes for combining consequence, vulnerability, and threat information to produce a comprehensive, systematic, and rational assessment of national, sector, and individual asset, system, or network risk.

Figure ES-1: NIPP Risk Management Framework

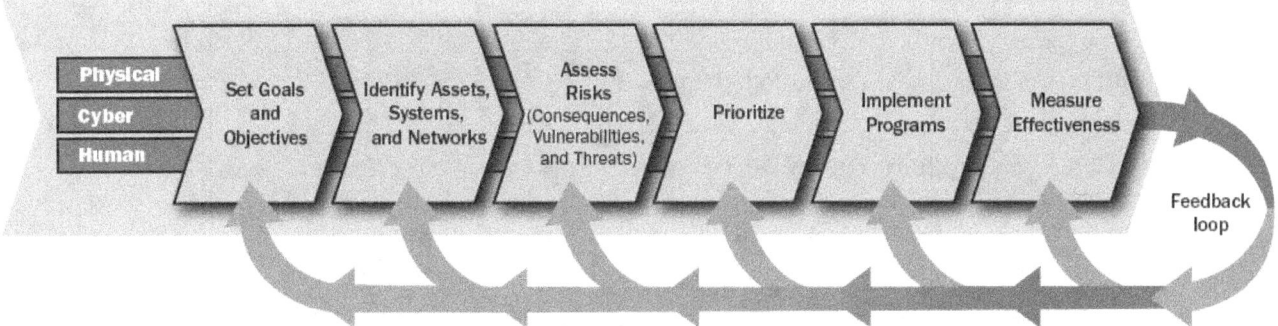

Continuous improvement to enhance protection of CIKR

Within the Critical Manufacturing Sector, many different methodologies have been and continue to be used by Critical Manufacturing facility owners and operators to assess the risks associated with their facilities. While individual owners have in many cases completed asset-, system-, or network-specific assessments on their own initiative, there has not been any sector-wide risk assessment for Critical Manufacturing. Due to the nature of the sector, the current economic climate, and the wealth of existing tools and mechanisms for assessing vulnerabilities at the facility level, the sector has decided to initially focus on a sector-wide risk assessment. To this end, the Critical Manufacturing SSA will actively seek the voluntary participation of all CIKR partners and other relevant stakeholders to design a risk assessment approach that facilitates such a sector-wide assessment. The SSA will work with all sector partners and request their input to update, refine, or develop the methodologies that can be useful in supporting this effort within the sector.

As identified in the NIPP base plan, risk assessments have several essential features and core elements that identify the characteristics and information needed to produce results for cross-sector risk comparisons. Essential features are that the risk assessment be documented, objective, defensible, and complete. Core elements include criteria based on the consequence, vulnerability, and threat components of the assessment, including physical, human, and cyber considerations. The SSA will work with all sector partners to ensure that the sector-wide risk assessment approach is both compliant with these criteria and tailored to the characteristics of the Critical Manufacturing Sector.

4. Prioritize Infrastructure

Even with all of the resources of the United States, it is not possible to protect every element of infrastructure against every possible type of terrorist attack, manmade incident, or natural disaster. Consequently, the Nation's CIKR protection program must prioritize protection across sectors in order that public resources are applied where they offer the most benefit for reducing risk. Using a systematic and consistent way of prioritizing assets also offers transparency and increases the defensibility of decisions regarding resource allocation by both the public and private sectors. Similar principles apply within individual CIKR sectors as well, and protection efforts must be prioritized within the Critical Manufacturing Sector to maximize the benefits of the limited resources available to the sector.

The sector prioritization process will involve aggregating, combining, and analyzing risk assessment results to determine which assets or systems face the highest risk (i.e., the most critical assets/systems). This process will lead to a comprehensive picture of risk for the Critical Manufacturing Sector and will allow the corresponding prioritization of protection measures. This process also will provide the basis for understanding the risk mitigation benefits, which, along with costs, are used to support protection planning and the informed allocation of resources. The prioritization process therefore involves two related activities. The first determines which assets or systems are exposed to the greatest risk. These will be assigned the highest priority in the development of risk management programs. The second activity determines which protective actions are expected to provide the most practical and cost-effective mitigation of risk.

5. Develop and Implement Protective Programs and Resiliency Strategies

The next step in the risk management framework is the development and implementation of protective programs and resiliency strategies for the sector. A protective program is a coordinated plan of action to prevent, deter, and mitigate all-hazards incidents on CIKR, and to respond to and recover from such natural disasters, terrorist attacks, or other incidents as quickly and effectively as possible. Resiliency strategies include actions taken to ensure the continued operation and activity of the sector even in the face of an incident.

The Critical Manufacturing Sector has developed an overarching approach to increase resiliency and prevent, deter, and mitigate disruption of the sector by manmade threats or natural disasters. This approach applies to individual protective programs that focus on physical, cyber, and human elements within the sector.

The sector will focus on protective and resiliency measures that are proportional to the risk (i.e., threat, vulnerability, and consequence) and are:

- Consistent with effective business practices and shared among stakeholders using industry and trade association communication mechanisms;
- Based on cost-sharing incentives, market systems, and other means that will encourage private sector participation;
- Built upon current practices that have proved to be effective;
- Applicable across assets while allowing owners and operators to select the most appropriate protective measure for their particular needs;
- Reliant on self assessments, where appropriate; and
- Simple to implement with low cost and high effectiveness.

Many Critical Manufacturing Sector infrastructure owners and operators have already implemented various protective measures for their assets, systems, and networks. For instance, many Critical Manufacturing Sector owners and operators have robust physical (access control, barriers), cyber (firewalls, security plans, limited access), and human (training, screening of personnel) protective measures in place within their organizations. Accordingly, additional protective program development must carefully consider the existing accomplishments of the sector. The approach outlined in the subsequent chapters necessitates carefully balancing the need for protection as well as various constraints facing program implementation.

6. Measure Effectiveness

The NIPP requires a metrics-based system of performance evaluation to establish accountability, document performance, facilitate diagnoses, and promote effective management. The metrics supply the data needed to measure progress toward specific goals and to show what corrective actions may be required to stay on target.

The foundation of measuring progress in sector activities is through assessing the effectiveness of Risk Mitigation Activities (RMA). RMAs are programs, tools, initiatives, projects, major tasks, or other undertakings that directly or indirectly lead to a reduction in risk. The NIPP performance measurement process requires all sectors to assess the success of CIKR protection efforts through developing metrics based upon key RMAs undertaken by the sector. Developing the specific list of RMAs and the associated key RMAs and metrics is performed by mapping existing protective activities of the sector against the risk landscape and protective priorities. From this initial list, those activities that are deemed to have the highest potential impact on mitigating sector risks will be labeled "key."

Using Metrics for Continuous Improvement. By using metrics responses to compare performance to goals, the Critical Manufacturing Sector can adapt its protection approach to account for progress achieved, as well as for changes in the threat and other relevant environments. At the national level, DHS and other Federal partners will use metrics to focus attention on areas of CIKR protection that warrant additional resources or other changes. If a comparison of performance against goals using information obtained through the metrics process reveals that there is insufficient progress, DHS and these partners will undertake actions to focus efforts on addressing those particular areas of concern.

7. CIKR Protection Research and Development

Science and technology offer considerable promise in helping to develop efficient and cost-effective ways of assessing risk and vulnerabilities, identifying potential threats, and protecting CIKR in the Critical Manufacturing Sector. DHS will work closely with the CMGCC, CMSCC and other sector partners on an annual basis to develop a research and development (R&D) strategy to support Critical Manufacturing Sector CIKR protection efforts. As part of the SSP development process, DHS has begun the steps for the creation of the first such Critical Manufacturing Sector R&D plan.

To develop a sector R&D plan, DHS will employ the following broad steps:

1. Identify sector R&D requirements;

2. Identify current R&D initiatives;

3. Map the current R&D initiatives to the sector R&D requirements to determine where gaps exist; and

4. Develop plans for creating R&D initiatives to fill the identified gaps.

During the development of the Critical Manufacturing Sector R&D plan, all nine themes identified in the National Critical Infrastructure Protection R&D plan will be assessed to determine whether activities in those areas potentially could benefit Critical Manufacturing Sector CIKR protection efforts.

8. Managing and Coordinating SSA Responsibilities

For many CIKR sectors, including the Critical Manufacturing Sector, developing and implementing a national plan to coordinate sector protective activities is a challenge. Chapter 8 of the SSP details many of the management and coordination activities that must be performed in order for the sector to meet this challenge. Included therein is a discussion of the annual reporting process, the resources and budgets allocated to sector CIKR protection efforts, sector training and education, sector information sharing, and information protection mechanisms.

Sector-Specific Plan Governance and Coordination. DHS is assigned the responsibility for managing and coordinating CIKR protection in the Critical Manufacturing Sector, including leading development of this SSP. Within DHS, this responsibility has been delegated to the Sector-Specific Agency Executive Management Office (SSA EMO), located in the Office of Infrastructure Protection within the National Protection & Programs Directorate.

Within the SSA EMO, a specific branch has been established to coordinate all Critical Manufacturing SSA management activities. The Critical Manufacturing Sector branch chief works closely with the CMGCC and CMSCC to chart the future direction and course of the sector's CIKR protection and resiliency efforts. The SSA EMO will evaluate its program management structure periodically to ensure that it provides the most effective means of meeting its SSA responsibilities.

Much like the NIPP, the Critical Manufacturing SSP is a living document and will undergo a thorough triennial review. The SSP will also be updated on an annual basis as warranted by changes in the sector's protective posture or processes. To ensure accuracy and reinforce the partnership nature of this effort, DHS will coordinate with the CMSCC and CMGCC on all updated and revised versions of the SSP.

Introduction

The Department of Homeland Security (DHS) was established officially as an executive department of the United States with the enactment of the Homeland Security Act of 2002. The act assigns DHS the responsibility of developing a comprehensive national plan for securing the Nation's critical infrastructure[1] and key resources (CIKR) and of recommending "measures necessary to protect the key resources and critical infrastructure of the United States in coordination with other agencies of the Federal Government and in cooperation with State and local government agencies and authorities, the private sector, and other entities."

Protecting the CIKR of the United States is essential to the Nation's security, public health and safety, economic vitality, and way of life. Attacks on CIKR could lead to significant disruption of the functioning of government and business alike and produce cascading effects far beyond the targeted sector and physical location of the incident. Direct terrorist attacks and natural, manmade, or technological hazards could produce catastrophic losses in terms of human casualties, property destruction, and economic effects, as well as profound damage to public morale and confidence. Attacks using components of the Nation's CIKR as weapons of mass destruction could have even more devastating physical and psychological consequences.

The national approach for CIKR protection is provided through the unifying framework established in Homeland Security Presidential Directive 7 (HSPD-7). This directive establishes the U.S. policy for "enhancing protection of the Nation's CIKR" and mandates a national plan to actuate that policy. In HSPD-7, the President designates the Secretary of Homeland Security as the "principal Federal official to lead CIKR protection efforts among Federal departments and agencies, State and local governments, and the private sector." HSPD-7 identifies 17 CIKR sectors[2] in recognition that each sector possesses unique characteristics and operating methods and assigns responsibility for CIKR sectors to designated Sector-Specific Agencies (SSAs).

A comprehensive and well-coordinated protection strategy for all CIKR sectors is an essential component of the homeland security mission to make America safer, more secure, and more resilient to terrorist attacks and other natural and manmade hazards. The National Infrastructure Protection Plan (NIPP) fulfills this important requirement by providing a coordinated approach to CIKR protection roles and responsibilities for Federal, State, local, tribal, territorial, and private sector partners. In the NIPP context, protection efforts include actions to detect, deter, mitigate, or neutralize the threat, vulnerability, or consequences associated with a terrorist attack or other incident.

Protection can include a wide range of activities, including hardening of facilities, building resiliency and redundancy, incorporating hazard resistance into initial facility design, initiating active or passive countermeasures, installing security systems, promoting personnel surety programs, and implementing cybersecurity measures. The NIPP provides the framework for

---

[1] See the Glossary of Terms for definitions of terms used in this document.
[2] Critical Manufacturing was identified as the 18th CIKR sector by the Secretary of Homeland Security in 2008.

the unprecedented cooperation that is needed to develop, implement, and maintain a coordinated national effort that brings together government at all levels, the private sector, and international organizations and allies.

A fundamental objective of the NIPP is to identify and protect infrastructure that is deemed *most critical*. Along with its complementary Sector-Specific Plans (SSPs), the NIPP provides a consistent, unifying structure for integrating both existing and future CIKR protection efforts within and across all sectors. It also provides the core processes and mechanisms to enable government and private sector partners to work together in implementing CIKR protection initiatives. The purpose of the SSPs is to detail the application of the NIPP risk management framework to each of the 18 CIKR sectors.

1. Sector Profile and Goals

The Critical Manufacturing Sector is crucial to the economic continuity and prosperity of the United States of America (U.S.). In 2006, the U.S. Census Bureau's Manufacturing and Construction Division reported that the U.S. manufacturing industry, relative to the taxonomy used by the Department of Homeland Security (DHS) for Critical Manufacturing, employed 1.1 million people and contributed $676 trillion to the economy.

Coordinating critical infrastructure protection activities within the Critical Manufacturing Sector requires a basic understanding of the nature and complexity of the sector itself. This chapter includes a detailed sector profile describing the classification of sector assets and cyber infrastructure (section 1.1); major Federal, State, local, and private sector partners and their relationship with DHS (section 1.2); and a listing of the sector goals (section 1.3).

1.1 Sector Profile

The Critical Manufacturing Sector is extremely diverse and encompasses several different functional activities, each of which produces a variety of products and materials. By examining the value chain and the services that support it, Critical Manufacturing Sector infrastructure can be divided based on four key functional areas: (1) Primary Metals Manufacturing, (2) Machinery Manufacturing, (3) Electrical Equipment Manufacturing, and (4) Transportation and Heavy Equipment Manufacturing. Each of these key functional areas depends upon physical, cyber, and human elements to perform their missions. Physical elements include the facilities that support each functional area. Human elements include the personnel associated with each of the functions. Finally, cyber elements include electronic systems for processing the information necessary for management and operation or for automatic control of physical processes.

Each key functional area has unique markets, assets, business models, and competitive conditions that shape their risk profile. However, there are several underlying characteristics of today's manufacturing environment that are common across each of the key functional areas within the Critical Manufacturing Sector. Examples include:

1. Most manufacturing enterprises are integrated into complex, interdependent supply chains.

Few businesses operate independently. Nearly all manufacturers are part of a chain of suppliers, vendors, partners, integrators, contractors, and customers that link to other industries and businesses. The reliability of these supply chains influences the competitive and risk profile that each company faces. To manage risk, companies maintain supply and product inventories, work with networks of suppliers and customers, and use financial instruments to hedge economic conditions.

2. Supply chains have been optimized for productivity and efficiency.

Competitive pressures cause businesses to optimize their manufacturing processes through highly coordinated business arrangements that enable manufacturers to maintain low inventories of raw materials and intermediate and end products.

3. Manufacturers have become highly reliant on global information and communication systems.

Automation, control, information processing, robotics, telecommunications, and the Internet have radically improved industrial productivity and have reshaped the operations and asset base of manufacturers.

4. Globalization and outsourcing have linked U.S. manufacturers with foreign suppliers, vendors, and customers through highly interdependent supply networks.

Manufacturers have increasingly turned to foreign markets for raw materials, component manufacturing, equipment and machinery, labor, and customers as a way to reduce overall costs. Highly sophisticated global supply networks have been created that can deliver quality goods quickly and at very low costs.

5. Manufacturers rely heavily on energy sources for heat, power, and raw materials.

While all businesses are dependent on energy, manufacturers typically require large amounts of these resources, much of it in the form of hard-to-store electricity and natural gas.

1.1.1 Primary Metals Manufacturing

Primary Metals Manufacturing converts raw materials into assemblies, intermediate products, and end products. Products may include sheet metal, bar stock, I-beams, slabs, or pipes. Primary Metals Manufacturing assets, systems, and networks typically include manufacturing facilities, processing and distribution facilities, sales offices and corporate headquarters, and product storage. Primary Metals Manufacturing includes iron and steel mills and ferro-alloy manufacturing; alumina and aluminum production and processing; and non-ferrous (copper, lead, etc.) metal production and processing.

1.1.2 Machinery Manufacturing

Machinery Manufacturing includes engine, turbine, and power-transmission equipment manufacturing. Machinery Manufacturing assets, systems, and networks typically include manufacturing facilities, processing and distribution facilities, sales offices and corporate headquarters, and product storage.

1.1.3 Electrical Equipment Manufacturing

Electrical Equipment Manufacturing includes specialized equipment, assemblies, intermediate products, and end products for power generation such as transformers, electric motors and generators, and industrial controls. Electrical Equipment Manufacturing assets, systems, and networks typically include manufacturing facilities, processing and distribution facilities, sales offices and corporate headquarters, and product storage.

1.1.4 Transportation and Heavy Equipment Manufacturing

Transportation Equipment Manufacturing includes auto and truck manufacturing, aerospace product and parts manufacturing, railroad rolling stock manufacturing, and other transportation equipment manufacturing. Heavy Equipment Manufacturing includes earth moving, mining, agricultural, construction, and other heavy material handling equipment. Transportation and Heavy Equipment Manufacturing assets, systems, and networks typically include manufacturing facilities, processing and distribution facilities, sales offices and corporate headquarters, and product storage.

1.1.5 Interdependencies and Overlapping Relationships With Other CIKR Sectors

Many Critical Manufacturing assets, systems, and networks are dependent on elements of other CIKR sector assets, systems, and networks to maintain functionality. In some cases, a failure in one sector will have a significant impact on the ability of another sector to perform necessary functions. It is extremely important to identify dependencies and interdependencies at asset, system, or network levels. Careful identification of dependencies and interdependencies is critical to understanding the consequences of a successful attack or natural disaster on infrastructure and identifying the manner in which incidents affecting other infrastructure could impact an interdependent asset, system, or network.

Internal Interdependencies

Many of the functional areas of the Critical Manufacturing Sector depend upon each other for goods and materials critical to sector activities. Manufacturing requires the use of often-complicated machinery and processes that depend upon specialized systems and equipment. For instance, the intermediate and end products of the Primary Metals Manufacturing functional area may be required to manufacture end products in the Machinery Manufacturing functional areas.

External Interdependencies

The Critical Manufacturing Sector is dependent on many other sectors to maintain full functionality. It relies on technology solutions from the Information Technology and Communications Sectors to support performance, operation, and communication through all aspects of the Critical Manufacturing industry value chain. The sector is also highly dependent on rail, trucking, and pipeline services for the secure transport of its products. For instance, manufacturing facilities depend upon transportation to deliver raw materials to, and end products from, their manufacturing centers. Conversely, many industries are reliant on the Critical Manufacturing Sector to provide the materials and products needed to perform their own functions.

Overlaps exist where assets, systems, and networks fit into more than one of the 18 CIKR sectors based on their characteristics or functions. It is important to identify overlaps at the sector level both to minimize the duplication of effort by overlapping SSAs and to ensure that infrastructure is not being ignored as a result of overlapping. In addition to mapping dependencies and interdependencies, table 1-1 describes the overlap between the Critical Manufacturing Sector and other CIKR sectors.

Table 1-1: Critical Manufacturing Sector Dependencies, Interdependencies, and Overlaps with Other CIKR Sectors

Sector (SSA)	Dependency/Interdependency/Overlap With the Critical Manufacturing Sector
Transportation Systems (DHS)	The CM Sector overlaps with, and is dependent on, the Transportation Systems Sector with regard to the transportation of materials by land, water, and air. Modes of transportation used to ship products in various stages of the value chain include ships, barges, trains, trucks, airplanes, and pipelines. Harm to the Transportation Systems Sector has the potential to seriously hinder the movement of materials and products and cause cascading effects throughout the CM Sector and its customers.
Energy (Department of Energy)	As with most other CIKR sectors, the CM Sector is dependent on the Energy Sector for power. An interruption to the power supply would directly affect all CM facilities located in the region serviced by the downed electric grid, and that interruption could potentially have cascading effects onto other CM facilities that are dependent on goods or materials provided by the directly affected facilities.
Emergency Services (DHS)	All CIKR sectors, including the CM Sector, rely on the Emergency Services Sector for response to incidents involving sector facilities. Conversely, the Emergency Services Sector depends upon the CM Sector to provide a variety of equipment critical to its mission.
Information Technology (DHS)	Like all other CIKR sectors, the CM Sector is dependent on the Information Technology Sector. Many CM Sector facilities rely heavily on information technology to manage day-to-day operations at their facilities, including facility security. Additionally, information technology is used by DHS and the CM Sector to disseminate security and threat information.

Sector (SSA)	Dependency/Interdependency/Overlap With the Critical Manufacturing Sector
Defense Industrial Base (Department of Defense)	The Defense Industrial Base Sector relies on the CM Sector for many inputs critical to defense industrial base products. Additionally, there is some overlap between the two sectors due to the nature of many Defense Industrial Base components, which may include manufacturing of some kind. Finally, due to the Defense Production Act, heavy industrial and manufacturing facilities may significantly alter their manufacturing processes and products should the country be mobilized for war.
Communications (DHS)	Like all other CIKR sectors, the CM Sector depends on the Communications Sector for much of its communications capability. Even though an interruption in communications would not be catastrophic to the CM Sector, damage to the Communications Sector would impact the CM Sector's ability to operate and would probably cause some cascading economic damages.
Chemical (DHS)	The CM Sector overlaps with and is dependent upon the Chemical Sector with regard to the chemicals used in all functional areas of the CM Sector. Chemicals are used in various stages of the value chain that range from the mining of raw materials to the chemicals required to operate manufactured end products. Examples of the types of chemicals used in everyday manufacturing include, but are not limited to solvents, passive acids, and paints.

1.2 CIKR Partners

Figure 1-1: Sector Partnership Model

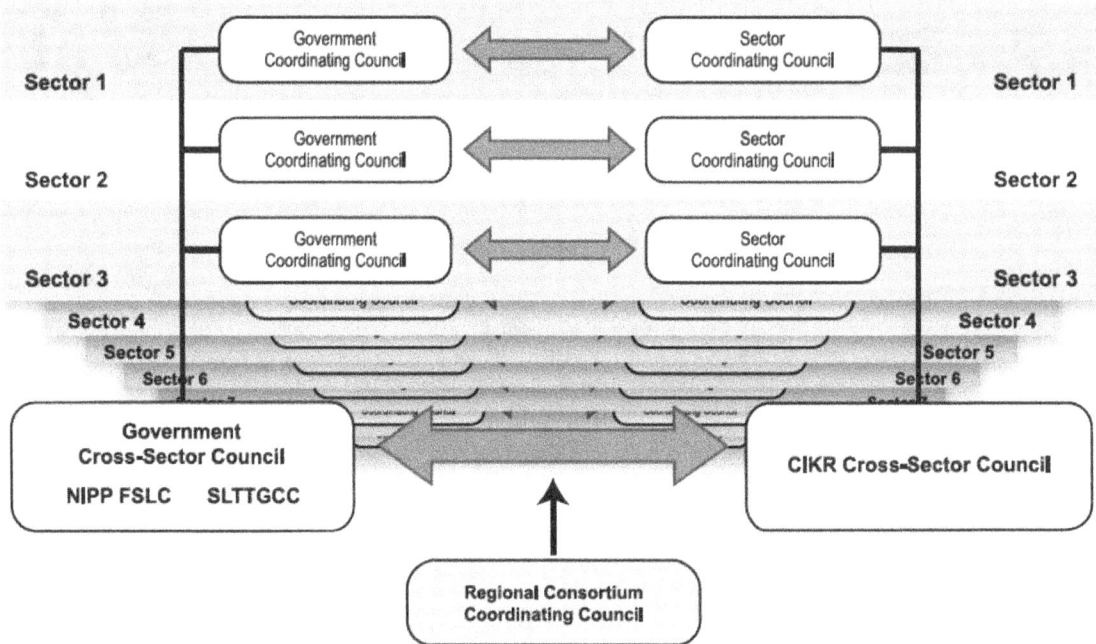

A variety of entities play different roles in helping secure each CIKR sector, including all levels of government, the private sector, academia, and others. Throughout the NIPP and the CIKR protection realm, these entities often are referred to as "CIKR partners" or "sector partners." This subsection provides a brief description of each of the key Critical Manufacturing Sector partners.

1.2.1 DHS/SSA

DHS is the SSA for the Critical Manufacturing Sector. As the SSA, DHS has numerous responsibilities, including leading, integrating, and coordinating the overall national effort to enhance Critical Manufacturing Sector CIKR protection and resilience. Some of the specific responsibilities that DHS has as the SSA include:

- Identifying, prioritizing, and coordinating the protection of sector-level CIKR with a particular focus on CIKR that could be exploited to cause catastrophic health effects or mass casualties comparable to those produced by a weapon of mass destruction;

- Managing the overall process for building partnerships and leveraging CIKR protection expertise, relationships, and resources within the sector, including sector-level oversight and support of the sector partnership model;

- Coordinating, facilitating, and supporting comprehensive risk assessment/management programs for high-risk CIKR, identifying protection priorities, and incorporating CIKR protection activities as a key component of the all-hazards approach to domestic incident management within the sector;

- Facilitating the sharing of real-time incident notification, as well as CIKR protection best practices and processes, and risk assessment methodologies and tools within the sector;

- Promoting sector-level CIKR protection education, training, and awareness in coordination with State, local, tribal, territorial, regional, and private sector partners;

- Informing the annual Federal budget process based on CIKR risk and protection needs in coordination with partners and allocating resources for CIKR protection accordingly;

- Monitoring performance measures for sector-level CIKR protection and NIPP implementation activities to enable continuous improvement and reporting progress and gaps to DHS;

- Contributing to the annual National Critical Infrastructure Protection Research and Development Plan;

- Identifying/recommending appropriate strategies to encourage private sector participation;

- Supporting DHS-initiated data calls to populate the Infrastructure Data Warehouse, enable national-level risk assessment, and inform national-level resource allocation;

- Supporting protocols for the Protected Critical Infrastructure Information Program;

- Working with DHS to develop, evaluate, validate, or modify sector-specific risk assessment tools;

- Supporting sector-level dependency, interdependency, consequence, and other analysis as required;

- Coordinating sector-level participation in the National Exercise Program, Homeland Security Exercise and Evaluation Program, and other sector-level activities;

- Assisting sector partners in their efforts to organize and conduct protection and continuity-of-operations planning, and elevate awareness and understanding of threats and vulnerabilities to their assets, systems, and networks;

- Assisting sector partners in their efforts to identify and promote effective sector-specific CIKR resiliency and protection practices and methodologies;

- Identifying and implementing plans and processes for enhancements in protective measures that align to all-hazards warnings, specific threat vectors as appropriate, and each level of the Homeland Security Advisory System;

- Understanding and mitigating sector-specific cyber risk by developing or encouraging appropriate protective measures, information-sharing mechanisms, and emergency recovery plans for cyber assets, systems, and networks within the sector and interdependent sectors; and

- Supporting DHS and Department of State efforts to integrate U.S. CIKR protection programs into the international and global markets, and address relevant dependency, interdependency, and cross-border issues.

Within DHS, SSA responsibilities have been delegated to the Office of Infrastructure Protection's (IP) Sector-Specific Agency Executive Management Office (SSA EMO).

1.2.2 Other Federal Departments and Agencies

Homeland Security Presidential Directive 7 (HSPD-7) charges DHS with primary responsibility for coordinating security in the Critical Manufacturing Sector; however, numerous other Federal departments and agencies have responsibilities that are integral to the overall security of the sector. To efficiently and effectively perform necessary CIKR protection activities in the Critical Manufacturing Sector, DHS and these other interested agencies must work together in a coordinated manner. Historically, this coordination was maintained through numerous formal and informal partnerships between DHS and the various pertinent Federal departments and agencies. As part of the NIPP, Government Coordinating Councils (GCCs) for each sector serve as the formal entity for coordinating government-led sector CIKR protection activities. The Critical Manufacturing Government Coordinating Council (CMGCC) is described in detail in section 8.3.1.1.

1.2.3 State, Local, Tribal, and Territorial Governments

State, local, tribal, and territorial authorities are integral to protecting our Nation's infrastructure. They constitute the front line of defense for our Nation's infrastructure and serve as or in close proximity to the owners or operators of CIKR. Of particular importance in the effort to secure our Nation are State, local, tribal, and territorial public-safety agencies, such as law enforcement, fire/rescue, emergency medical services, and emergency management personnel. It is of great importance that DHS and the Critical Manufacturing Sector have a strong, cooperative relationship with these and other important State, local, tribal, and territorial agencies.

DHS has established the State, Local, Tribal, and Territorial Government Coordinating Council (SLTTGCC) to ensure there is a forum for State, local, tribal, and territorial government representatives to engage with the Federal Government and the CIKR owners and operators within the sector partnership model. The Council reviews Federal plans and policy, engages stakeholders, and contributes to the efforts of each of the CIKR sectors. The SLTTGCC membership, which is made up of Homeland Security Advisors or their equivalent, participates in GCC and Sector Coordinating Council (SCC) meetings for many sectors, ensuring the State and local perspective is present at these meetings between the Federal Government and the private sector. DHS IP also interacts regularly with State and local government officials through the Protective Security Advisor Program.

In addition to DHS's relationship with State, local, tribal, and territorial governments, private sector entities historically have worked closely with those agencies. Specifically, many members of the Critical Manufacturing Sector have engaged in cooperative emergency response planning, drilling, and exercises with local responders for more than 20 years. Many Critical Manufacturing facilities are also part of local mutual assistance networks, an integral part of a local area's emergency response system.

1.2.4 Private Sector

Infrastructure owners and operators play a central role in CIKR protection. Within the Critical Manufacturing Sector, the private sector owns and operates the vast majority of the infrastructure. As a result, the private sector is an integral CIKR partner in efforts to secure the Critical Manufacturing Sector. In addition to ownership and management of most Critical Manufacturing

Sector infrastructure, the private sector is uniquely situated to provide the following important contributions to CIKR protection in the Critical Manufacturing Sector:

- Implementation of a strong base of existing security initiatives on which CIKR partners can build to enhance sector protection and resiliency;

- Expertise to address and support cybersecurity efforts, through their individual companies, membership in the SCC, participation in the SCC Cyber Working Group, and the Cross-Sector Cybersecurity Working Group;

- Visibility into CIKR assets, systems, networks, facilities, functions, and other capabilities;

- Ability to take actions to respond to incidents;

- Ability to innovate and to provide products, services, and technologies to quickly focus on requirements; and

- Existing, robust mechanisms useful for sharing and protecting sensitive information regarding threats, vulnerabilities, countermeasures, and best practices.

1.2.4.1 Critical Manufacturing Sector Coordinating Council

The Critical Manufacturing Sector Coordinating Council (CMSCC) includes manufacturing companies that are critical to the Nation's economy, both domestically and internationally. The CMSCC's structure aligns with HSPD-7's goal of protecting the Nation from terrorist attacks and natural disasters that could "damage the private sector's capability to ensure the orderly functioning of the economy and delivery of essential services; have a negative effect on the economy through the cascading disruption of other critical infrastructure and key resources; or undermine the public's morale and confidence in our national economic and political institutions."

The CMSCC, for this purpose, shall include private sector manufacturing companies and firms of any size that comprise U.S. critical infrastructure and/or provide key resources, or that are considered iconic representatives of the U.S. economy. At a minimum, it will be representational of "critical manufacturing" industries as identified in section 1.1.

The Council will serve as the primary liaison between the Critical Manufacturing Sector and the United States government at all levels concerning policy, strategy, and planning issues as outlined by the Council's Mission.

1.2.5 Advisory Councils

Advisory councils provide advice, recommendations, and expertise to the government regarding CIKR protection policy and activities. These entities also help enhance public-private partnerships and information sharing. They often provide an additional mechanism to engage with a pre-existing group of private sector leaders to obtain feedback on CIKR protection policy and programs, and to solicit suggestions to increase the efficiency and effectiveness of specific government programs. Examples of CIKR protection-related advisory councils include:

- **Critical Infrastructure Partnership Advisory Council (CIPAC):** The CIPAC is a partnership between the Federal Government and private sector CIKR owners and operators to facilitate effective coordination of Federal CIKR protection programs pursuant to section 121 of the Homeland Security Act and HSPD-7. The private sector members of the CIPAC are the members of the various CIKR SCCs, and the public sector members are DHS and the other members of the corresponding GCCs. DHS has exercised its authority under section 871 of the Homeland Security Act to exempt the CIPAC from the Federal Advisory Committee Act (FACA). (See Federal Register (FR) 14930 (March 24, 2006).) This ensures that the CIPAC members can discuss security-sensitive topics without the risk that these discussions could become public and jeopardize security. The CIPAC can meet as a whole, or in the form of joint committees specific to a particular sector.

- **Homeland Security Advisory Council (HSAC):** The HSAC provides advice and recommendations to the Secretary of Homeland Security on relevant issues. The Council members, appointed by the Secretary, include experts from State and local governments, public safety, security and first-responder communities, academia, and the private sector.

  - Private Sector Senior Advisory Committee (PVTSAC): The Secretary of Homeland Security established the PVTSAC as a subcommittee of the HSAC to provide the HSAC with expert advice from leaders in the private sector. An example of the type of activities undertaken by the PVTSAC is the authoring of an HSAC report titled *Homeland Security Information Sharing Between Government and the Private Sector* (August 2005).

- **National Infrastructure Advisory Council (NIAC):** The NIAC provides the President, through the Secretary of Homeland Security, with advice on the security of physical and cyber systems across all CIKR sectors. The Council is comprised of up to 30 members appointed by the President. Members are selected from the private sector, academia, and State and local governments. The Council was established (and amended) under Executive Orders 13231, 13286, and 13385.

1.2.6 Academia, Research Centers, and Think Tanks

The academic and research center communities play an important role in enabling national-level CIKR protection and implementation of the NIPP, including:

- Establishing Centers of Excellence (i.e., university-based partnerships or federally funded R&D centers) to provide independent analysis of CIKR protection issues;

- Supporting the research, development, testing, evaluation, and deployment of CIKR protection technologies;

- Analyzing, developing, and sharing best practices related to CIKR protection efforts;

- Researching and providing innovative thinking and perspective on threats and the behavioral aspects of terrorism;

- Preparing or disseminating guidelines, courses, and descriptions of best practices for physical security and cybersecurity;

- Developing and providing suitable risk analysis and risk management courses for CIKR protection professionals; and

- Conducting research to identify new technologies and analytical methods that can be applied by CIKR partners to support the NIPP efforts.

Many of these same activities could be of use to efforts to secure the Critical Manufacturing Sector. DHS, as the SSA, will work with other Critical Manufacturing Sector partners to determine how academia, research centers, and think tanks can be leveraged to help enhance the sector's protective posture.

1.2.7 International Organizations and Foreign Countries

The Critical Manufacturing industry is a global industry with many domestic facilities both receiving raw materials, intermediate products, and equipment from foreign sources and supplying raw materials, intermediate products, and end products to foreign customers. For instance, steel manufacturing companies may import pig iron from Brazil, convert the pig iron into steel, and export the steel to Canada. Additionally, Critical Manufacturing has considerable international elements, including facilities located in countries around the globe. An attack or disaster that affects foreign facilities or systems may result in direct or indirect consequences felt in the U.S. As a result, certain foreign entities are Critical Manufacturing Sector partners and will be engaged, as appropriate, to address certain aspects of sector risk.

1.3 Sector Goals and Objectives

Sector goals state the comprehensive protective posture that the government and infrastructure owners and operators are working together to achieve for the sector. Such goals reflect the overall risk management outcomes that the Critical Manufacturing SSA, CMSCC, and CMGCC seek to produce. While involving all CIKR partners in the creation of sector goals would be ideal, the size and diversity of the sector makes such a task infeasible. While the members of the CMSCC represent the major functional areas of the sector, they do not represent every single business contained in the Critical Manufacturing Sector. Moreover, while the CMSCC exists as the primary representative body for private sector interests in the sector with regard to CIKR protective activities, it cannot commit the sector to any specific mission, vision, goals, objectives, or milestones. As a result, the mission, vision, goals, objectives, and milestones contained in this CM SSP represent a collaborative but non-binding strategy that outlines the future activities of the Critical Manufacturing SSA, CMSCC, CMGCC, and other sector partners.

Figure 1-2: Sector Goals

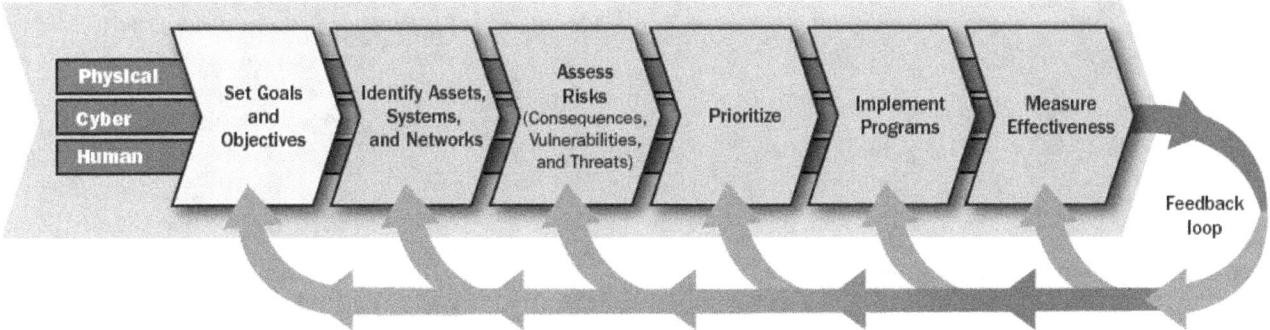

Continuous improvement to enhance protection of CIKR

1.3.1 Critical Manufacturing Sector Mission Statement

DHS, in collaboration with the CMSCC, has developed the following Mission Statement:

Mission Statement for the Critical Manufacturing Sector

Reduce risks to the Critical Manufacturing Sector through proactive prevention, preparation for and mitigation of natural and man-made threats leading to effective response and recovery through public-private partnership.

1.3.2 Critical Manufacturing Sector Goals

Based upon the Critical Manufacturing Sector Mission Statement, the sector has developed the following five goals:

Goals for the Critical Manufacturing Sector

Goal 1: Achieve an understanding of the assets, systems, and networks that comprise the critical infrastructure of the Critical Manufacturing Sector.

Goal 2: Develop an up-to-date risk profile of the assets, systems, and networks within the Critical Manufacturing Sector that will enable a risk-based prioritization of protection activities.

Goal 3: Develop protective programs and resiliency strategies that consider the physical, human, and cyber elements of sector infrastructure and address sector risk without hindering economic viability.

Goal 4: Create a means of measuring the progress and effectiveness of Critical Manufacturing Sector CIKR protection activities.

Goal 5: Develop processes for ensuring appropriate and timely information sharing between government and private sector partners in the Critical Manufacturing Sector.

1.3.3 Critical Manufacturing Sector Objectives

Based upon the Critical Manufacturing Sector Goals, the sector has developed the following objectives that contribute to achieving the goals.

Goal 1 Objectives

- Identify critical assets of each of the sector's functional areas.

- Identify and annually review Critical Manufacturing Sector functional areas, including human, physical, and cyber components that support the Nation's security, economy, public health, and safety.

Goal 2 Objectives

- Assess and prioritize risks to sector functional areas, including evaluating emerging threats and vulnerabilities, and mapping them to the infrastructure to prioritize protective efforts.

- Tailor risk methodologies to accommodate sector diversity.

Goal 3 Objectives

- Tailor protective measures, which mitigate associated consequences, vulnerabilities, and threats, to accommodate the diversity of the sector.

- Develop and share security best practices and protective measures with CIKR partners.

- Identify plans, protocols, and procedures to reduce recovery time for Critical Manufacturing Sector functions following an incident.

- Identify and ensure the availability of resources (pre- and post-incident) that are critical to the sector's effective recovery following an incident.

- Improve the capabilities of public and private sector CIKR partners to respond to emerging, man-made, and natural threats.

Goal 4 Objectives

- Develop metrics that allow for measurement of effectiveness of sector CIKR protection efforts and a means of gathering the requisite information for measuring effectiveness that is not unduly burdensome on asset owners and operators or other partners.

- Develop a means for reporting on CIKR protection effectiveness to relevant partners throughout Federal, State, and local governments, as well as the private sector.

Goal 5 Objectives

- Foster collaborative communications processes between Critical Manufacturing Sector partners.

- Improve situational awareness during normal operations, developing situations, and actual incidents in the sector.

- Collaborate, develop, and share appropriate threat and vulnerability information among public and private sector partners, including development of indications and warnings.

- Develop and maintain incident response and coordination plans and procedures.

- Participate in exercises for the purpose of validating communication protocols, response plans, and procedures.

1.4 Value Proposition

DHS seeks the active, voluntary, and full engagement of all CIKR partners, particularly private sector owners and operators. DHS can achieve this only if all participants recognize the business value of their participation. Key areas of value are:

- Minimizing service disruption to ensure consistent, predictable revenue flow;

- Resiliency and restoration of disrupted services to provide a competitive advantage; and

- Public recognition for preparedness, continuity of service, and good corporate citizenship to maintain and enhance corporate reputations with investors, customers, and potential employees.

The importance of Critical Manufacturing Sector contributions to accomplishing critical national responsibilities makes CIKR partners' full and visible engagement an important goal for DHS. Through active participation, partners will receive improved access to information regarding vulnerabilities and threats, as well as risk assessment and risk-reduction best practices. This information will enhance the capability to respond to critical business and customer requirements.

2. Identify Assets, Systems, and Networks

This chapter describes the steps that will be taken to identify and gather pertinent information on the assets, systems, and networks that compose the Critical Manufacturing Sector, including information on the physical, cyber, and human elements of those pieces of infrastructure (see figure 2-1).

Figure 2-1: Identify Assets, Systems, and Networks

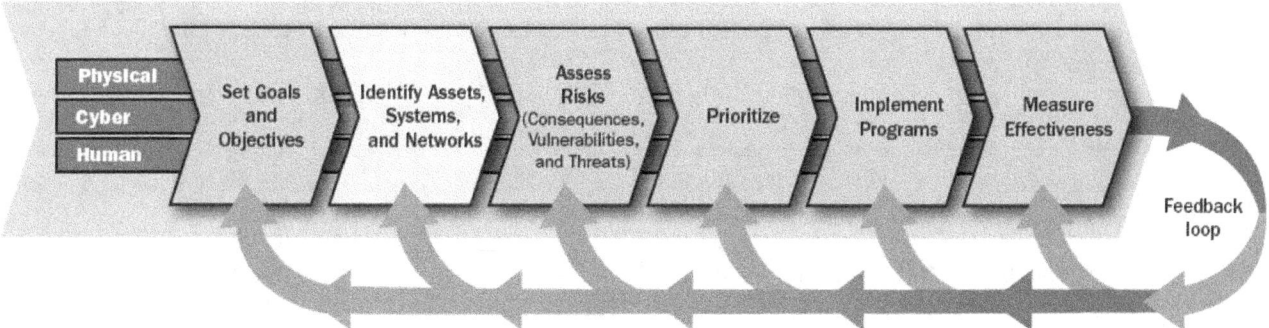

Continuous improvement to enhance protection of CIKR

As a primary method of gathering information on the assets, systems, and networks of the Critical Manufacturing Sector, DHS will continue to leverage previously initiated data-collection efforts, including continued coordination with Federal, State, and local entities. DHS will work with the CMSCC and CMGCC both to review current methods of data collection and to identify and discuss other potential means for data collection that may be more efficient or encompassing, or less expensive, than current data-collection methods.

DHS utilizes a distributed IT architecture to integrate existing data sets from Federal, State, and commercial sources into a virtual federated database, the Infrastructure Data Warehouse (IDW). This architecture allows numerous CIKR partners to maintain and verify data on sector infrastructure, reduces duplication of effort and distributes information management, and provides access to a more robust and complete data set that retrieves information from multiple noncontiguous databases.

The major steps used to identify assets, systems, and networks, as well as infrastructure of significance, are:

- **Develop Criteria:** Identify a method, means, equation, or process to determine what is of significance, based on consequences, vulnerability, and threat (thus risk).

- **Validate Criteria:** Ensure the methods or processes identify the information requirements needed to conduct the analysis.

- **Collect Data:** Collect that information by: (1) reviewing existing tools or databases to determine if they have the correct data, or (2) investigating other potential sources (i.e., Federal agency, private entity) to collect the required information. Information collected should adhere to data standards to facilitate information exchange with other partners, customers, or sources.

- **Apply Criteria to Collected Data:** Once information is collected, conduct analysis to determine what is significant.

DHS has specific approaches and processes to collect appropriate asset, system, and network data and to identify critical functionality. Processes should include descriptions of mechanisms for making data collection efforts more manageable, such as:

- Prioritizing the approach for data outreach to different CIKR partners;

- Identifying, reviewing, and using existing databases;

- Supporting State, local, tribal, and territorial entities in identifying and gathering the types of information that should be collected because of the relevance of the information to potentially high-risk or critically important infrastructure; and

- Identifying specific assets, systems, or networks (or classes of them) for which additional data collection is unnecessary because they are associated with inherently low risk.

As the SSA for the Critical Manufacturing Sector, DHS will help identify and obtain appropriate data for assets, systems, and networks that play a vital role in the Nation's security or economy, particularly those that involve significant dependencies, interdependencies, or critical functionality. Data collection, compilation, and storage efforts must ensure that data content, accuracy, currency, and formats are standardized. The IDW provides a coordinated and consistent framework to incorporate and display the data submitted by local, State, and Federal departments and agencies; the private sector; and integrated Federal or commercial databases.

Much of the information gathered as part of implementing the Critical Manufacturing SSP is sensitive from either a business or security perspective; therefore, the security and privacy of the data are of the utmost importance. Protection of this information is described both in section 4.3 of the NIPP Base Plan and in section 8.4.2 of this document. Processes for verifying and updating this information also are described in this document.

Additional interagency coordination efforts involving multi-jurisdictional programs will be required to complete the identification of the sector's assets, systems, and networks. DHS will work with sector partners to refine the taxonomy used to categorize sector assets. DHS and the SSAs will also continue to work with Federal, State, local, and tribal governments, as well as the private sector, to ensure that the IDW is accurate, complete, and secure.

2.1 Defining Information Parameters

Due to the dynamic nature of the risk environment, and continuously evolving priorities and information requirements, the SSA anticipates that information collection parameters will change over time. As the sector conducts its risk assessment, and as DHS further develops its own infrastructure information needs, the SSA will work closely with sector partners to determine categories of information that may need to be collected. The following serve as potential information categories that may be collected to contribute to Critical Manufacturing Sector protection efforts:

- Name, address, and local contact information of the asset;

- Geographic location (e.g., latitude/longitude, global positioning system (GPS) coordinates, distance to nearest major metropolitan area);

- Owner/operator name, address, and type (e.g., public, private);

- 24-hour emergency contact person and toll-free number;

- Physical structure information (e.g., square footage, seating capacity, number of floors, building height);

- Business identification codes and ratings (e.g., North American Industry Classification System (NAICS) Codes, Environmental Protection Agency Facility Identification, Dun and Bradstreet rating);

- Cyber elements (e.g., distributed control systems (DCS), process control systems (PCS), supervisory control and data acquisition (SCADA) systems; access control databases);

- DHS program information (e.g., Protective Security Advisor district; Buffer Zone Plan (BZP) status);

- Regulated or hazardous materials products produced or stored onsite;

- Annual production quantity of regulated or hazardous products;

- Primary consumers of products;

- Region/service area (e.g., Midwest, South, international);

- Active access to Homeland Security Information Network (HSIN)-Critical Manufacturing;

- Impact on sectors (both Critical Manufacturing and other CIKR sectors) in case of loss or failure;

- Existing protective measures;

- Population distribution in the area surrounding the facility;

- Imagery and spatial data of the area surrounding the facility;

- Structures and lines of sight to the facility; and

- Other critical assets in the area surrounding the facility.

2.2 Collecting Infrastructure Information

2.2.1 Historical DHS Infrastructure Information Collection Efforts

Historically, DHS has used a variety of means for gathering data on the Nation's infrastructure. In 2004, and since, DHS issued data calls to State Homeland Security Offices asking the States to identify CIKR located within its borders. Similarly, as part of Project Matrix, DHS requested information from other Federal agencies in an effort to collect data on facilities located throughout the Nation. In addition to these broad data calls, DHS has coordinated with individual governmental entities to gain access to critical infrastructure information collected in response to statutory and other requirements.

In addition to working with States and other Federal entities, DHS has collected asset data by working directly with asset owners and operators. During the implementation of various initiatives, such as BZPs or Site Assistance Visits, DHS learns valuable information concerning high-risk critical infrastructure directly from asset owners and operators, local law enforcement, and other emergency response personnel. Similar information is garnered when DHS and asset owners and operators work together to tactically respond to specific threat intelligence and assist in protecting select facilities. The knowledge acquired about CIKR during both strategic and tactical operations performed by DHS is catalogued and maintained in the IDW.

2.2.2 Future DHS Infrastructure Information Collection Efforts Within the Critical Manufacturing Sector

Going forward, DHS's primary means for collecting data on Critical Manufacturing Sector assets will be through combining partial functions of the NADB with the IDW with additional sector partner input and validation as needed. This process will enable DHS to (1) identify facilities that present a high level of risk, (2) support the determinations of preliminary and final rankings for high-risk facilities, (3) assess a facility's security vulnerabilities, and (4) evaluate a facility's security plan to address vulnerabilities.

2.2.3 Privacy of Data

Because much of the information gathered as part of the NIPP risk-management effort is sensitive either from a business or a security perspective, protection of the information and the privacy of the data are of utmost importance, and DHS takes its information-protection responsibilities very seriously. Mechanisms for ensuring protection of this information are described both in section 4.3 of the NIPP and in section 8.4.2 of this SSP.

2.3 Verifying Infrastructure Information

DHS will work with organizations undertaking voluntary efforts to identify those facilities where independent verification of data has already occurred. The SSA will coordinate with CMSCC partners to verify existing information and ensure its accuracy and relevance. Additionally, the SSA will coordinate with CMSCC and CMGCC partners to verify and ensure accurate responses to all infrastructure information requests.

2.4 Updating Infrastructure Information

CIKR partners may be asked to update their profiles whenever a significant change[3] occurs at their facilities, be it in a facility's operating characteristics or in a facility's protective posture (e.g., assessments completed, webcams installed). Updated data will be provided to DHS in the same way the original data were submitted.

---

[3] To date, what constitutes a "significant change" that would warrant an update of infrastructure information has not yet been defined. DHS will work with the CMSCC and other sector partners to determine the parameters for what changes should be considered significant.

3. Assess Risks (Consequences, Vulnerabilities, and Threats)

Risk assessments create a comprehensive picture of the sector's overall exposure to risk. As defined in the NIPP, the risk management framework for CIKR protection assesses risk as a function of consequence, vulnerability, and threat.

Consequence: The effect of an event, incident, or occurrence; reflects the level, duration, and nature of the loss resulting from the incident.

Vulnerability: Physical features or operational attributes that render an entity open to exploitation or susceptible to a given hazard.

Threat: Natural or manmade occurrence, individual, entity, or action that has or indicates the potential to harm life, information, operations, the environment, and/or property.

The process outlined in the sections below illustrates how the Critical Manufacturing Sector will incorporate these aspects of consequence, vulnerability, and threat into a risk assessment methodology that will measure the risks to the Critical Manufacturing Sector.

Figure 3-1: Assess Risks (Consequences, Vulnerabilities, and Threats)

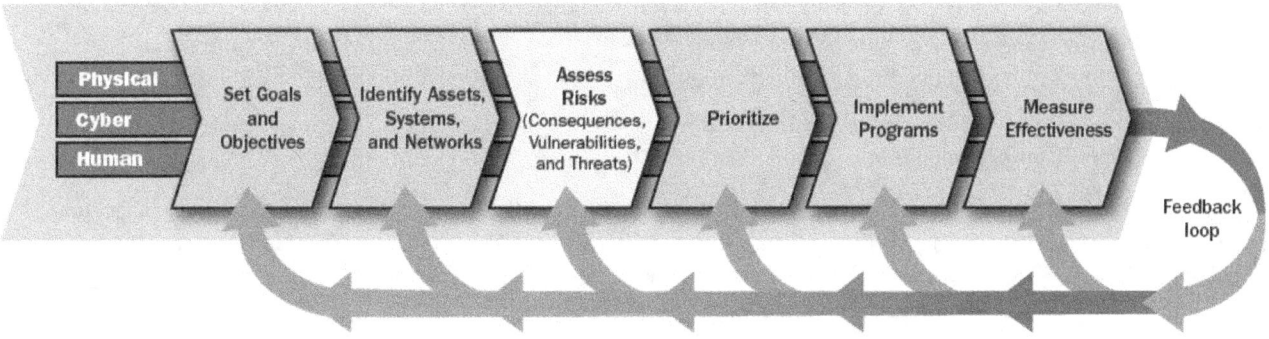

Continuous improvement to enhance protection of CIKR

3.1 Use of Risk Assessment in the Sector

While individual owners have in many cases completed asset-, system-, or network-specific assessments on their own initiative, there has not been any sector-wide risk assessment for Critical Manufacturing. Due to the nature of the sector, the current economic climate, and the wealth of existing tools and mechanisms for assessing vulnerabilities at the facility level, the sector has decided to initially focus on a sector-wide risk assessment. To this end, the Critical Manufacturing SSA will actively seek the voluntary participation of all CIKR partners and other relevant stakeholders to design a risk assessment approach that facilitates such a sector-wide assessment. The SSA will work with all sector partners and request their input to update, refine, or develop the methodologies that can be useful in supporting this effort within the sector.

The Critical Manufacturing Sector has a long history of development and application of methodologies for assessing risk and prioritizing assets to be protected. Such methodologies have been developed by a variety of sector partners, including individual companies; professional and trade associations; academic institutions; and research centers. Because of the diversity of the sector, the specific risk assessment methodologies used vary significantly. Various methodologies, including Failure Modes and Effects analyses, Hazard and Operability studies, and others, are used to determine risk (or assess vulnerabilities and/or consequences) to specific facilities, systems, supply chains, or other discrete components of the sector's infrastructure. The SSA will work with all sector partners to identify existing risk (or consequence, threat, or vulnerability) tools and methodologies that may contribute to developing a sector-wide risk assessment.

The broad range of methods used by the Critical Manufacturing Sector is also a result of the international scope of the sector's assets, supply chains, and products. Many Critical Manufacturing companies are global and have extensive experience in dealing with a wide variety of natural and manmade threats. As such, they often have very sophisticated methodologies for prioritizing investments based on risk. These methodologies have also highlighted the importance of interdependencies within Critical Manufacturing as well as among the other CIKR sectors.

The subsequent sections outline the approach for the Critical Manufacturing Sector's sector-wide risk assessment. This outline reflects the initial approach of the Critical Manufacturing Sector based upon the input of CMSCC members in partnership with the SSA. The Critical Manufacturing Sector views the below approach as a dynamic process that may change as sector partners implement the risk assessment steps.

3.1.1 Process for Assessing Risks

The sections below describe the individual steps in the risk methodology that the Critical Manufacturing Sector has developed. The sector has chosen to break down the components of the sector as a whole into the functional areas defined in sections 1.1.1 through 1.1.4. These functional areas will undergo an initial screening and analysis to determine those components that warrant additional attention. Once the components have been identified, the sector will conduct an analysis consisting of a combination of consequence, vulnerability, and threat information to arrive at a baseline of risk information.

It is important to note that this outline is intended as the first effort toward risk assessment by the Critical Manufacturing Sector. The sector anticipates that as the risk assessment is conducted, the associated methodology and processes will evolve and may change from what is presented below.

As identified in the NIPP, risk assessments have several essential features and core elements that identify the characteristics and information needed to produce results for cross-sector risk comparisons. Essential features are that the risk assessment be documented, objective, defensible, and complete. Core elements include requirements based on the consequence, vulnerability, and threat components of the assessment. The approach outlined below incorporates each of these essential features and core elements.

3.2 Screening Infrastructure

In light of the dispersion of the Critical Manufacturing Sector throughout the Nation, its many facilities or systems that may pose little or no security risk, and the limited resources available to address CIKR protection therein, it is neither practical nor financially responsible to seek comprehensive vulnerability and risk assessments for each sector facility or system. Thus, as a precursor to the performance of any sector-wide risk assessment efforts, screening will occur to identify those assets or systems that may warrant the expenditure of resources necessary for detailed vulnerability and risk assessments.

A comprehensive sector-wide risk assessment approach requires careful consideration of the diverse nature of the Critical Manufacturing Sector. Due to this unique nature, the Critical Manufacturing Sector has developed an approach that follows three steps:

• The sector will define the functional areas that make up Critical Manufacturing, currently: Primary Metals Manufacturing, Machinery Manufacturing, Electrical Equipment Manufacturing, and Transportation and Heavy Equipment Manufacturing.

• The sector will conduct an analysis of each functional area to determine whether there are organizations that control the market share to the degree that their incapacitation would result in nationally significant consequences based upon the criteria outlined in section 3.3.

• In addition to identifying functional areas, the Critical Manufacturing Sector will conduct an analysis of each functional area to identify whether there are critical suppliers of materials who, if incapacitated, could result in the aforementioned consequences.

3.3 Assessing Consequences

The risk methodology for the Critical Manufacturing Sector will assess consequences based upon the four general categories set forth in the NIPP, namely:

• **Public Health and Safety Impact:** Effect on human life and physical well-being (e.g., fatalities, injuries);

• **Economic Impact:** Direct and indirect effects on the economy (e.g., cost to rebuild the asset, cost to respond to and recover from attack, downstream costs resulting from the disruption of products or services, and long-term costs due to environmental damage);

• **Psychological Impact:** Effect on public morale and confidence in national economic and political institutions; or

• **Impact on Government:** Effect on the government's ability to maintain order, deliver minimum essential public services, ensure public health and safety, and carry out national security-related missions.

Furthermore, the Critical Manufacturing Sector will evaluate the consequences in each of these general categories through analysis of parameters illustrated in table 3-1. The combined categories will be weighted accordingly to determine the final risk ranking. Due to the nature of the Critical Manufacturing Sector, it is predicted that Economic Impact will be the most significant category of consequences and form the foundation of the analysis.

Table 3-1: Critical Manufacturing Sector Consequence Analysis Parameters

1. Public Health and Safety Impacts	3. Psychological Impacts
a. Affected population	a. Iconic/symbolic assets
b. Fatalities	b. High-profile and/or symbolic casualties
c. Acute injuries/illnesses	
2. Economic Impacts	**4. Impact on Government**
a. Asset replacement costs	a. Military mission importance
b. Remediation costs	b. Cross-sector impacts
c. Business interruption costs	
d. National/regional economic importance/multiple sector impact	

3.4 Assessing Vulnerabilities

Vulnerabilities are the characteristics of an asset, system, or network's design, location, security posture, process, or operation that render it susceptible to destruction, incapacitation, or exploitation by mechanical failures, natural hazards, terrorist attacks, or other malicious acts. Vulnerability assessments identify areas of weakness that could result in consequences of concern, taking into account intrinsic structural weaknesses, protective measures, resiliency, and redundancies.

Historically, the Critical Manufacturing Sector has utilized assessment methodologies, including Fault Tree Analyses, Process Hazards Analyses, and others to identify vulnerabilities affecting its assets and systems. However, no single vulnerability tool or assessment methodology is universally applicable. Individual manufacturing companies use assessment tools that may be developed by professional and trade associations, Federal organizations, government laboratories, and private sector firms. There exists a wide variety of tools, and many facilities or systems in the Critical Manufacturing Sector have already undergone assessments using one or more of these.

To meet the overarching goal of sector-wide risk assessment, the Critical Manufacturing SSA will seek the collaboration of all CIKR partners and other relevant stakeholders to identify a methodology for assessing vulnerabilities that affect risk. Furthermore, common and emerging sector vulnerabilities will be assessed continuously through periodic discussions among the Critical Manufacturing SSA, the CMGCC, and the CMSCC, including classified discussions when necessary. Vulnerabilities also will be identified through the reporting of incidents and through R&D efforts.

In particular, the Critical Manufacturing Sector risk methodology will look to identify vulnerabilities on two distinct levels. First, the methodology will consider those characteristics of the sector as a whole that might constitute vulnerabilities. For instance, the sector's reliance upon a complex and international supply chain may constitute a vulnerability that stretches across all functional areas. Second, the methodology will examine any specific assets or systems that are identified through the risk methodology as warranting particular attention and examine whether those individual assets or systems possess vulnerabilities that may impact the sector.

To address vulnerability assessments specific to cybersecurity, the SSA, in coordination with the DHS National Cyber Security Division (NCSD) and the CMSCC, will promote the use of a Cyber Security Evaluation Tool that combines two voluntary cybersecurity assessment tools to raise awareness of cybersecurity issues.

The Cybersecurity Vulnerability Assessment (CSVA) tool assesses the policies, plans, and procedures in place to reduce cyber vulnerability and presents options for consideration for managing cyber risk. The tool provides a flexible and scalable assessment for business and control systems and leverages various recognized standards, guidance, and methodologies.

Additionally, the SSA provides information on the Control Systems Cyber Security Self-Assessment Tool (CS2SAT) to interested companies. The CS2SAT incorporates and utilizes a comprehensive set of cybersecurity recommendations based on available and emerging standards in the control systems community. This information is incorporated into the tool and provides an interface for users to systematically retrieve requirements specific to their control system network. The CS2SAT provides an excellent means to perform a self-assessment of the risk posture of a control system environment.

3.5 Assessing Threats

The third variable in the risk equation is threat. Determining terrorist threat, however, is beyond the scope of most non-Federal (and many Federal) entities. Consequently, most asset owners and operators must rely on threat input from DHS to accurately calculate the risk associated with a given asset. However, it is important to note that risks to the Critical Manufacturing Sector are not limited to terrorist actions. Natural disasters also pose a significant threat, as do cyber attacks, malicious insiders, and industrial accidents; all will be carefully considered in the Critical Manufacturing risk methodology.

The DHS Homeland Infrastructure Threat and Risk Analysis Center (HITRAC) serves as a national center for the integration, analysis, and sharing of information regarding the threat of terrorist attacks against U.S. infrastructure. HITRAC coordinates with DHS, other Federal departments and agencies, the intelligence community, State and local governments, law enforcement agencies, and the private sector. In addition to developing and providing a General Threat Environment document to each sector, DHS shares terrorist threat information via classified threat briefings to members of the Critical Manufacturing Sector who possess security clearances. At these briefings, various Federal agencies will brief the private sector representatives on general and specific threats associated with the Critical Manufacturing Sector, as well as information on the overall threat of terrorism to the Nation.

In addition to providing both classified and unclassified general threat information to Critical Manufacturing Sector partners, DHS will share, upon receipt, specific threat information regarding particular facilities with the targeted facility owners and operators. This will allow DHS; the facility owner/operator; and other Federal, State, and local entities to implement an appropriate, coordinated response to the threat.

4. Prioritize Infrastructure

Even with all of the resources of the United States, it is not possible to protect every element of infrastructure against every possible type of terrorist attack, manmade incident, or natural disaster. Consequently, the Nation's CIKR protection program must prioritize protection across sectors in order that resources are applied where they offer the most benefit for reducing risk. Using a systematic and consistent way of prioritizing assets also offers transparency and increases the defensibility of the decisions that are made about resource allocation by both the public and private sectors. Similar principles apply within individual CIKR sectors as well, and protection efforts must be prioritized within the Critical Manufacturing Sector to maximize the benefits of the limited resources available to the sector.

Figure 4-1: Prioritize Infrastructure

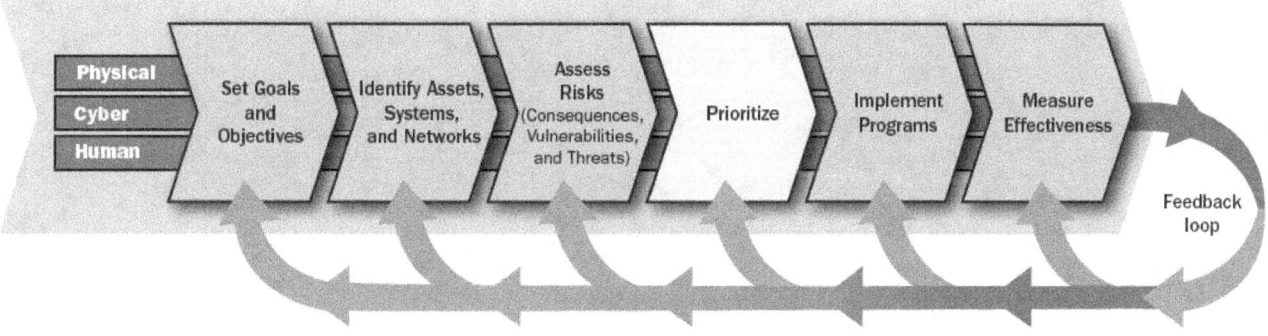

Continuous improvement to enhance protection of CIKR

Prioritizing infrastructure assets, systems, and networks is only one part of the prioritization piece. To allocate resources in the manner that most cost-effectively reduces risk, protective efforts (i.e., activities, measures, programs) must be assessed and prioritized. This provides decision makers with a second thread of information that can be used to make policy, funding, and other decisions regarding CIKR protection and allows the prioritization of assets and systems on a sector-wide basis, in addition to just individual facilities or functional areas.

This chapter of the document addresses the process used to normalize and prioritize the results of assessments of Critical Manufacturing facilities and related systems and networks. The process will be developed in a manner that allows the identification of assets, systems, and networks, both within the Critical Manufacturing Sector and across all CIKR sectors that are facing the greatest risks.

The sector prioritization process will involve aggregating, combining, and analyzing risk-assessment results to determine which assets or systems face the highest risk (i.e., the most critical assets/systems). This process will lead to a comprehensive picture of risk for the Critical Manufacturing Sector and will allow the corresponding prioritization of protection measures. This process also will provide the basis for understanding the risk-mitigation benefits, which, along with costs, are used to support protection planning and the informed allocation of resources. The prioritization process therefore involves two related activities. The first determines which assets or systems are exposed to the greatest risk. These will be assigned the highest priority in the development of risk management programs. The second activity determines which protective actions are expected to provide the most practical and cost-effective mitigation of risk.

The prioritization process for the Critical Manufacturing Sector requires the analysis and understanding of factors beyond mere asset-by-asset risk assessment results. Additional factors needed include the availability and cost of risk-reduction measures and their potential for success, existing legal and policy directives and constraints, and potential impacts of risk-reduction measures on facilities, companies, and the sector overall. These factors, combined with the underlying risk assessment results, provide the foundation for the prioritization process for the Critical Manufacturing Sector.

The process used to prioritize protective programs, which is based on a combination of their risk-reduction potential and their cost-effectiveness, is described in chapter 5, Develop and Implement Protective Programs and Resiliency Strategies.

5. Develop and Implement Protective Programs and Resiliency Strategies

Protective programs and resiliency strategies are coordinated plans of action to prevent, deter, and mitigate all hazards to CIKR, and to respond to and recover from such incidents as quickly and effectively as possible. Protective programs guide infrastructure owners and operators on the most effective strategies for protecting their assets, systems, and networks, given the general classes of threats, vulnerabilities, and consequences applicable to their infrastructure.

Figure 5-1: Develop and Implement Protective Programs

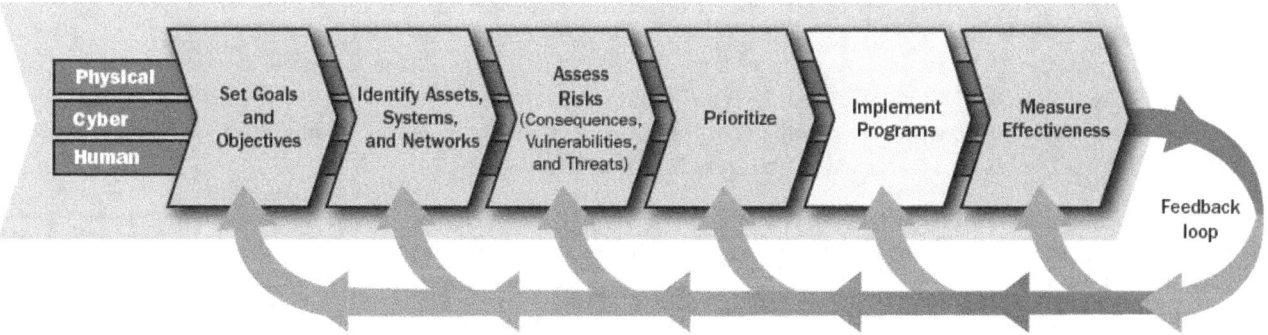

Continuous improvement to enhance protection of CIKR

5.1 Overview of Sector Protective Programs and Resiliency Strategies

The Critical Manufacturing Sector has developed an overarching program to increase resiliency and prevent, deter, and mitigate disruption of the sector by manmade threats or natural disasters. This approach applies to protective programs that focus on physical, cyber, and human elements within the sector.

The sector will focus on protective measures that are proportional to the risk (i.e., threat, vulnerability, and consequence) and are:

- Consistent with effective business practices and shared among stakeholders using industry and trade association communication mechanisms;

- Based on cost-sharing incentives, market systems, and other means that will encourage private sector participation;

- Built upon current practices that have proved to be effective;

- Applicable across assets while allowing owners and operators to select the most appropriate protective measure for their particular needs;

- Reliant on self-assessments, where appropriate; and

- Simple to implement with low cost and high effectiveness.

Many Critical Manufacturing Sector infrastructure owners and operators have already implemented various protective measures for their assets, systems, and networks. For instance, many critical manufacturing owners and operators have robust physical (access control, barriers), cyber (firewalls, security plans, limited access), and human (training, screening of personnel) protective measures in place within their organizations. A good example of a protective program in place in the sector is the Control Systems Security Program, which provides coordination among sector partners at all levels of government and the owner/operators of control systems, to improve the security of these systems within the sector and across all sectors. Accordingly, additional protective program development must carefully consider the existing accomplishments of the sector. The approach outlined in the subsequent sections necessitates carefully balancing the need for security as well as various constraints facing program implementation.

5.2 Determining Protective Program Needs

Given existing protective programs as well as those under development, the identification of additional protective programs requires a process that incorporates these pre-existing efforts while giving due consideration to risk, levels of protection, constraints, and the ultimate design and implementation of protective measures. Additionally, the Critical Manufacturing Sector recognizes that comprehensive security and resiliency programs require careful consideration of not only physical and human, but also cyber elements within the sector. In addition to common information technology infrastructures such as core business networks and communications equipment, the Critical Manufacturing Sector also relies on a wide variety of industrial control systems that manage physical processes through computer-interface means. The sector will collaborate with all relevant partners to examine the risk landscape as well as the cost/benefit associated with additional measures needed to increase sector resiliency, protect critical services, and ensure product delivery. The sector will decide which additional measures should be instituted and develop a strategy to distribute the costs associated with this effort.

Owners and operators recognize that disruption or destruction can have significant impacts on operational survivability, shareholder value, customer relations, and public confidence. However, security costs have grown considerably over recent years, and additional investments in protection contribute to those costs. Additional investments may not be considered necessary, particularly for events that owners and operators feel may never occur. Therefore, the protective measures developed by the Critical Manufacturing Sector will be grounded in an accurate risk-based assessment of the need for the measure and the threshold required for its implementation.

The following steps describe the process for implementing protective programs in the Critical Manufacturing Sector. Because of the dynamic nature of the threat environment and the diversity of the Critical Manufacturing Sector, this process may be refined on an ongoing basis.

STEP 1: Identify Risk

Effective protective programs require careful risk-based analysis that incorporates threats, vulnerabilities, and consequences. Chapters 3 (Assess Risk) and 4 (Prioritize Infrastructure) of this document go into further detail on the processes the Critical Manufacturing Sector will use to identify risk and prioritize infrastructure based on that risk. Risk identification, and the subsequent steps toward developing protective measures, will involve all relevant sector stakeholders associated with identified risks.

STEP 2: Determine Protective Measures to Mitigate Risk

After identifying risks and appropriate sector partners, the sector will identify potential protective measures that could mitigate the risk. These measures may include, but are not limited to: improved communications, information sharing, and industry-recognized best practices. Protective measures will be tailored to the identified risks while considering sector characteristics. Additionally, the sector will consider physical, human, and cyber elements when developing potential protective measures. Should the sector identify gaps that do not have any recognized solutions, these areas will be nominated for future research and development activities.

STEP 3: Identify Constraints to Implementing Protective Measures

Each protective measure identified will likely have some constraints that must be considered prior to implementation. Constraints may include physical characteristics, operational considerations, prohibitive cost, technology barriers, or other factors that could influence the ability to implement a protective program. Cost-benefit analyses are an integral part of identifying constraints, as there will always be more risks to the sector than there are resources to address them.

5.3 Protective Program Implementation

After determining the need for protective program implementation and developing targeted protective measures, the next step is implementation. Given the characteristics of the Critical Manufacturing Sector, the asset owner/operator will be responsible for implementing any selected protective measures on a voluntary basis. However, in conjunction with certain programs or pilot projects, DHS, other Federal agencies, State or local entities may be involved. This is much more likely with regard to assets that are identified as high-risk through the earlier stages of SSP implementation.

Typically, the asset owner/operator's business case will govern what measures are included in its overall protection program. As mentioned earlier, cost/benefit analysis is an important factor for the critical manufacturing industry when selecting protective programs and resiliency strategies for implementation. However, the industry is also well aware of the potential costs, including physical, economic, and human consequences, of neglecting protective measure implementation. Additionally, the sector recognizes that there may be some assets or systems that are so critical or may result in such high consequences that protective measures may be called for even if the asset or system is deemed to have low risk in light of current threats and hazards.

Finally, many organizations across all levels of government have existing protective programs that are available to Critical Manufacturing Sector owners and operators. DHS and other Federal entities have a wide variety of programs aimed at improving physical and cybersecurity, increasing awareness through training and education, and increasing information sharing between public and private partners. Prior to implementing new protective programs, the sector will carefully examine existing and planned programs that may be leveraged to improve protection at specific assets or across the sector.

5.4 Monitoring Program Implementation

Every time a protective measure is implemented, the protective posture changes for both the individual infrastructure where the protective measure is implemented and the sector as a whole. For subsequent protective decisions to be the most cost-effective, the protective posture of the affected asset needs to be reviewed and updated accordingly. For protective measures at high-risk infrastructure, or protective measures that for other reasons may alter the sector-wide protective picture, DHS may need to recalibrate its sector-wide analyses and adjust the overarching protective program accordingly. This is part of the overall measurement of performance for the Critical Manufacturing Sector, which represents the final step of the six-step NIPP risk management framework and is discussed in detail in the following chapter.

6. Measure Effectiveness

Figure 6-1: Measure Effectiveness

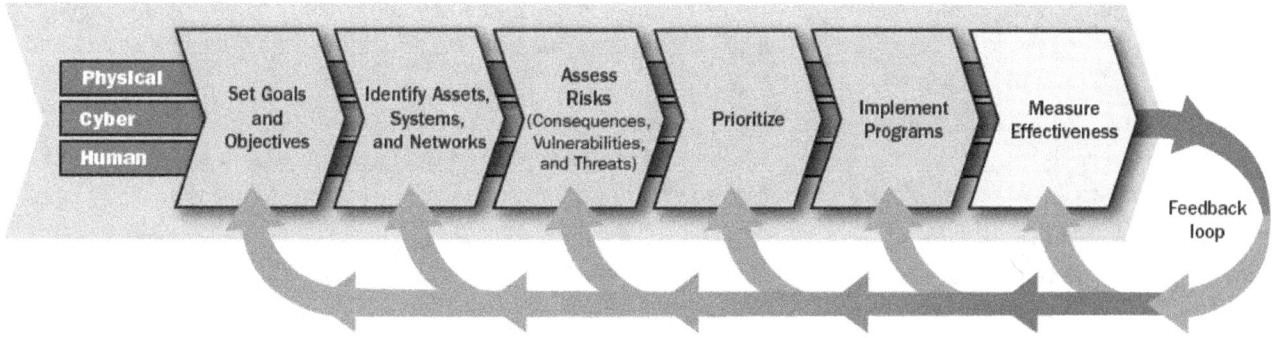

Continuous improvement to enhance protection of CIKR

The NIPP requires a metrics-based system of performance evaluation to establish accountability, document performance, facilitate diagnoses, and promote effective management. The metrics supply the data needed to measure progress toward specific goals and to show what corrective actions may be required to stay on target.

6.1 Risk Mitigation Activities

Risk Mitigation Activities (RMA) are programs, tools, initiatives, projects, major tasks, or other undertakings that directly or indirectly lead to a reduction in risk. The NIPP performance measurement process requires all sectors to assess the success of CIKR protection efforts through developing metrics based upon key RMAs undertaken by the sector. These are developed through a process similar to the process outlined in chapter 5. In some cases, however, RMAs may be drawn from existing programs and initiatives.

Developing the specific list of RMAs and the associated key RMAs and metrics is performed by mapping existing protective activities of the sector against the risk landscape and protective priorities outlined in chapters 4 and 5. From this initial list, those activities that are deemed to have the highest potential impact on mitigating sector risks will be labeled "key." Key RMAs initially identified include: implementing the NIPP sector partnership model; sponsoring security clearances for CM Sector members; attending Enhanced Critical Infrastructure Protection visits; and establishing the CM Sector portal on Homeland Security Information Network-Critical Sectors (HSIN-CS).

6.2 Process for Measuring Effectiveness

In order to ensure the effectiveness and continual improvement of Critical Manufacturing Sector programs and activities, the sector will work closely with the NIPP Measurement and Reporting Office to participate in the various processes for measuring the effectiveness of activities within the Sector Partnership Model.

6.2.1 Process for Measuring Sector Progress

The focus of the NIPP metrics program is on outcome metrics. Outcome metrics track progress toward a strategic goal by demonstrating beneficial results rather than tracking the level of activity. Effective performance measurement requires the cooperation of the owners and operators to work with the SSA to develop accurate responses to the metrics.

In addition to outcome metrics, other information will be utilized, such as output and descriptive data.

- **Output (or Process) Data** are used to gauge whether specific activities were performed as planned, track the progression of a task, or report on the output of a process. An example of process data may be the number of Critical Manufacturing distributors who performed vulnerability assessments in the previous year. Output data have an important role, showing progress made in performing the activities necessary to achieve CIKR protection goals. They also help build a comprehensive picture of CIKR protection status and activities.

- **Descriptive Data** are used to understand sector resources and activity, but they do not reflect CIKR protection performance. For instance, typical descriptive data would show the number of assets by asset class or owner type (e.g., number of Critical Manufacturing facilities, percent of Critical Manufacturing facilities owned by members of the private sector).

The Critical Manufacturing Sector anticipates that the initial metrics developed for sector RMAs will focus on output and descriptive data. However, as sector partnerships, collaboration, and activities mature, the metrics will evolve to focus on outcomes.

6.2.2 Collecting and Verifying Information

The SSA is responsible for collecting and verifying the data needed to measure and quantify progress in development and implementation of the risk management framework for the sector. The SSA will work with all CIKR partners to identify the most efficient and cost-effective process to collect the data required. Unless stated otherwise, metrics data will be collected annually. Data that may be sensitive or proprietary will be protected through established protocols.

DHS is responsible for evaluating and prioritizing the information provided by its CIKR partners. It will collaborate with the SSA and appropriate sector partners in assessing the relative risks of critical assets within the Critical Manufacturing Sector to determine the priorities for national risk-reduction programs based on an assessment of risk across all 18 CIKR sectors.

6.2.3 Reporting

The SSA is responsible for collecting and reporting data pertaining to the objectives and metrics. As required by HSPD-7, the SSA will provide an annual report to the Secretary of Homeland Security on progress in identifying, prioritizing, and coordinating protection of CIKR in the Critical Manufacturing Sector. This information will be developed in collaboration with the CMGCC and CMSCC and will be available for distribution throughout the sector. The Critical Manufacturing Sector Annual Report:

- Establishes a baseline of existing sector-specific CIKR protection priorities, programs, and initiatives against which future improvements will be assessed;

- Identifies sector priorities and out-year requirements with a focus on projected shortfalls in resources for sector-specific CIKR protection and for protection of CIKR within the sector that is deemed to be critical at the national level;

- Determines and explains how sector efforts support the national effort;

- Provides an overall progress report for the Critical Manufacturing Sector and measures that progress against the CIKR protection goals and objectives described in this SSP;

- Provides feedback to DHS, other CIKR sectors, and other government entities to provide the basis for the continuous improvement of the CIKR protection program; and

- Helps identify best practices from successful programs and shares these within and among CIKR sectors.

6.3 Using Metrics for Continuous Improvement

By using metrics responses to compare performance to goals, the Critical Manufacturing Sector can adapt its protection approach to account for progress achieved, as well as for changes in the threat and other relevant environments. At the national level, DHS and other Federal partners will use metrics to focus attention on areas of CIKR protection that warrant additional resources or other changes. If a comparison of performance against goals using information obtained through the metrics process reveals that there is insufficient progress, DHS and its partners will undertake actions to focus efforts on addressing those particular areas of concern.

Information gathered within the risk management framework process helps determine adjustments to specific CIKR protection activities. Accordingly, the sector and national risk profiles must be reviewed routinely to help inform current and prospective allocation of resources in light of recently implemented protective actions or other factors, such as increased understanding of potential system-wide cascading consequences or new threat intelligence. In addition to quantitative measures, qualitative feedback also will be used to augment and improve the effectiveness and efficiency of public and private sector CIKR protection programs. DHS works with sector partners to identify and share lessons learned and best practices for all aspects of the risk management process. By sharing such information, DHS and its sector partners can work to continuously improve CIKR protection efforts undertaken across the Critical Manufacturing Sector.

7. CIKR Protection Research and Development

7.1 Overview of Sector Research and Development (R&D) Approach

Science and technology enable the development of efficient and cost-effective ways of mapping potential consequences, identifying potential threats, assessing risk and vulnerabilities, and enhancing the resilience of Critical Manufacturing Sector infrastructure. The SSA will work closely with the CMSCC, CMGCC, and other sector partners to develop a focused R&D program to enhance the security of the sector and achieve its strategic goals. This collaborative approach will help to identify areas where R&D would be beneficial, identify R&D initiatives currently underway, and sponsor or actually perform R&D initiatives.

One of the seminal documents that will help guide this effort is the annual National Critical Infrastructure Protection (CIP) R&D Plan, which DHS Science and Technology (S&T) first developed in 2005 in coordination with the White House's Office of Science and Technology Policy. The National CIP R&D Plan is structured around nine themes:

1. Detection and sensor systems;

2. Protection and prevention;

3. Entry and access portals;

4. Insider threats;

5. Analysis and decision support systems;

6. Response, recovery, and reconstitution;

7. New and emerging threats and vulnerabilities;

8. Advanced infrastructure architectures and system designs; and

9. Human and social issues.

Within each of these major themes are distinct R&D focus areas. These have been carefully structured to be complementary, non-repeating, and supportive of other focus areas wherever possible, with constant consideration of the interrelationship between physical and cyber elements.

7.2 Sector R&D Requirements

The SSA will annually collaborate with sector partners to identify R&D requirements that have particular benefit to the Critical Manufacturing Sector. The SSA will work closely with DHS S&T, the CMSCC and CMGCC, and other relevant partners to discuss R&D requirements throughout the sector in a series of workshops. These workshops will invite sector owners and operators and CMGCC members to identify and prioritize R&D interests of value to the Critical Manufacturing Sector. These workshops will also consider the cyber needs and priorities of the sector when identifying R&D requirements to support the achievement of sector goals. In collaboration with these partners, the SSA will develop a list of R&D areas where the application of government resources, whether through existing or new products, could provide value.

7.3 Sector R&D Plan

Once sector R&D requirements are identified, the SSA will work with sector partners to identify which requirements may have solutions in early planning stages, partially developed, or fully developed through existing R&D initiatives across the Federal Government. Additionally, the workshops will identify a process for sponsoring or funding new R&D projects through potential public-private partnerships. As appropriate, the SSA will coordinate with relevant sector partners to involve subject matter experts and end users in existing or planned projects to ensure final products are tailored to the needs of the sector itself.

Additionally, the sector will establish a R&D Working Group to address sector R&D requirements and work with DHS S&T. S&T has established Integrated Product Teams (IPTs) to coordinate the planning and execution of R&D programs together with the eventual hand-off to maintainers and users of project results. The IPTs are critical nodes in the process to determine operational requirements, assess current capabilities to meet operational needs, analyze gaps in capabilities, and articulate programs and projects to fill in the gaps and expand competencies. The sector R&D Working Group will work closely with S&T to determine how sector subject matter experts can engage most effectively with the IPTs to ensure a final product that is tailored to the end user.

7.4 R&D Management Processes

The SSA, in collaboration with DHS S&T, will take the lead in monitoring sector R&D progress, assessing the impact of R&D efforts on sector goals, and updating this portion of the SSP. Throughout the process, the SSA will work closely with sector partners, including the CMSCC and CMGCC, to ensure evolving requirements and subject matter expertise are inserted as appropriate.

8. Managing and Coordinating SSA Responsibilities

For many CIKR sectors, including the Critical Manufacturing Sector, developing and implementing a plan that coordinates sector protective activities and improves sector resiliency is a new challenge. This chapter of the SSP details many of the management and coordination activities that will be performed by the SSA to meet this challenge. Specifically, this chapter will address: (1) how DHS will manage its SSA responsibilities; (2) the processes for maintaining and updating the SSP; (3) how sector annual reporting requirements related to CIKR protection will be satisfied; (4) resources and budgets of sector partners; (5) sector CIKR protection training and education; (6) implementation of the sector partnership model; and (7) how information will be shared and protected.

8.1 Program Management Approach

DHS is assigned the responsibility for managing and coordinating Critical Manufacturing CIKR protection activities, including leading development of this SSP. Within DHS, this responsibility has been delegated to the Sector-Specific Agency Executive Management Office (SSA EMO), located in the Office of Infrastructure Protection within the National Protection & Programs Directorate.

Within the SSA EMO, a specific branch has been established to coordinate all Critical Manufacturing SSA management activities. The Critical Manufacturing Sector branch chief works closely with the CMGCC and CMSCC to chart the future direction and course of the sector's CIKR resiliency efforts. The SSA EMO will evaluate the structure of its program management periodically to ensure that it is the most effective means of meeting its SSA responsibilities.

The Critical Manufacturing SSA will:

- Serve as the focal point for all DHS responsibilities related to Critical Manufacturing Sector CIKR protection;
- Coordinate and manage development, implementation, maintenance, and modification of the Critical Manufacturing SSP;
- Fulfill the SSA responsibilities as described in this SSP; and
- Collaborate with other DHS entities concerning other sector efforts described within this SSP.

In performing its responsibilities, the Critical Manufacturing branch will work with fellow DHS entities to leverage programs being performed throughout the Department that help reduce risk in the sector.

8.2 Processes and Responsibilities

8.2.1 SSP Maintenance and Update

The Critical Manufacturing SSP is a living document and, as such, needs to be maintained and updated on an ongoing basis. Like the NIPP, the SSP will undergo a thorough review that includes collaboration with the CMSCC, CMGCC, and other sector partners on a triennial basis. In addition to the formal triennial review, the Critical Manufacturing Sector will review and update the document on an ad hoc basis (annually at a minimum), as warranted by changes in the sector's protective posture or procedures. All revised versions of the SSP will be collaborative products based on input from CMSCC and CMGCC partners to ensure accuracy and full engagement in the sector partnership model.

8.2.2 SSP Implementation Milestones

The SSA has developed a series of implementation actions designed to facilitate the achievement of the goals and objectives outlined in the SSP. The actions included in the matrix are the shared responsibilities for SSP implementation and the sector partners with primary responsibility for each of the actions are identified. Milestones are specified in terms of the number of days after the release of the SSP or by a specific date. Actions are organized by SSP chapter to provide a ready reference to the information provided in the SSP.

In the implementation milestones matrix, only those sector partners with primary responsibility for a given task have been identified; however, virtually all partners have at least a supporting role in every implementation action listed.

Table 8-1: SSP Implementation Milestones Matrix

Section	Implementation Actions	Milestone				CIKR Partner			
		NLT 90 Days After SSP Release	NLT 180 Days	NLT 365 Days	Specific Date	DHS	Other Federal Agencies	State, Territory, Locality, Tribe	Private Sector
1. Sector Profile and Goals									
	Annually review sector goals and objectives				Annual	X	X	X	X
	Annually review sector functional areas to ensure appropriate representation of Critical Manufacturing partners				Annual	X	X	X	X
2. Identify Assets, Systems, and Networks									
	Identify critical assets, systems, and networks of each of the sector's functional areas		X			X	X	X	X

Section	Implementation Actions	Milestone				CIKR Partner			
		NLT 90 Days After SSP Release	NLT 180 Days	NLT 365 Days	Specific Date	DHS	Other Federal Agencies	State, Territory, Locality, Tribe	Private Sector
	Identify taxonomy for Critical Manufacturing for use in the IDW		X			X			X
3. Assess Risks (Consequences, Vulnerabilities, Threats)									
	Review the Critical Manufacturing Sector risk profile	X				X			
	Begin development of the sector risk methodology		X			X	X	X	X
4. Prioritize Infrastructure									
	Review and refine as necessary the process for prioritizing sector infrastructure			X		X	X	X	X
5. Develop and Implement Protective Programs									
	Tailor existing protective measures proven in other sector programs to accommodate the diversity and nature of the Critical Manufacturing Sector		X			X	X	X	X
	Implement HSIN-CS as an information sharing platform that caters to the specific needs of all sector partners		X			X	X	X	X
6. Measure Progress									
	Participate in the metrics process required for each CIKR sector as defined in the NIPP				Annual	X			
7. CIKR Protection R&D									
	Develop and communicate requirements for CIKR-related R&D to DHS for use in the national R&D planning effort				Annual	X			X

Section	Implementation Actions	Milestone				CIKR Partner			
		NLT 90 Days After SSP Release	NLT 180 Days	NLT 365 Days	Specific Date	DHS	Other Federal Agencies	State, Territory, Locality, Tribe	Private Sector
8. Managing and Coordinating SSA Responsibilities									
	Ensure appropriate representation from government entities on the Critical Manufacturing Government Coordinating Council	X				X		X	
	Develop processes to share information among sector partners during an incident	X				X	X	X	X
	Develop and submit the Sector Annual Report				Annual	X			

8.2.3 Resources and Budgets

Due to the multitude of Federal, State, local, tribal, territorial, and private sector partners that contribute funds and other resources to protection of the Critical Manufacturing Sector, neither DHS nor any other single entity has authority over resources or budgets for the entire sector. As a result, DHS has limited insight into exactly how Critical Manufacturing partners allocate resources related to sector CIKR protection activities.

Within these limitations, the SSA will work with sector partners to gather available resource and budgetary information and develop sector-specific investment priorities. Based on the national priorities identified in the NIPP, National CIKR Protection Annual Report, and the Critical Manufacturing SSP, the DHS will develop and share recommendations regarding allocation of sector resources and related funding. These recommendations will be based on a coordinated approach to Critical Manufacturing Sector protection, and the recommendations made for specific resource or funding allocations will be informed by an analysis of cost effectiveness and risk reduction.

Regarding DHS resources and budgets, the SSA EMO, in conjunction with other DHS offices and divisions as appropriate, will develop the recommended annual budget requests for Critical Manufacturing Sector CIKR protection-related expenditures. The SSA EMO will submit its budget requests for the following fiscal year. Between September and November, DHS will work with the Office of Management and Budget (OMB) to make final decisions regarding the DHS budget and resources available for the Critical Manufacturing Sector.

Finally, in addition to managing resources allocated to DHS specifically for Critical Manufacturing protection and resiliency issues, the SSA, in collaboration with the CMGCC and CMSCC as appropriate, will serve as the SME to review and provide recommendations on specific targeted grant programs that may benefit the sector.

8.2.4 Training and Education

Implementation of the national risk management framework relies on building and maintaining individual and organizational CIKR protection expertise. Training and education at multiple levels and in a variety of areas are necessary to achieve and sustain this level of expertise. Section 6.2 of the NIPP contains a discussion of some of the areas of expertise where training is recommended, examples of types of training currently being offered, and other general information on CIKR protection-related training and education.

In addition to individual training, organizational training and exercises are integral to improving the sector's overall protective posture. Training all facility staff (not just security personnel) on how to identify suspicious activity could reduce dramatically the likelihood of a successful terrorist incident or its consequences. Red-teaming facilities (i.e., testing a facility's protective measures using trained teams of simulated adversaries) can help asset owners and operators determine the effectiveness of their protection programs and prepare staff to respond quickly and properly in the event of an actual incident. Tabletop exercises can provide similar results not only to asset owners and operators, but also to State and local law enforcement, DHS, and other Federal entities.

Many Critical Manufacturing Sector partners have already participated in a variety of the individual and organizational training and educational activities described above; however, more will be done. As part of the Critical Manufacturing SSP implementation process, the SSA will work with sector partners to identify and encourage participation in existing training and education opportunities. Additionally, the SSA will work with sector partners to identify any gaps in training or training opportunities and to develop ways to fill these gaps to ensure that the necessary training and educational opportunities and available to, and being used by, Critical Manufacturing Sector partners.

To foster preparedness and response in the sector, the SSA collaborates with sector partners during National Level Exercises (NLEs). These exercises provide the opportunity for sector partners to test information-sharing processes and incident management procedures, and provide valuable insight into cross-sector dependencies. The lessons learned from the NLE are incorporated by public and private sector partners into incident management procedures to increase sector preparedness and response in an all-hazards environment.

The sector is also an active participant in NLEs that are focused solely on cybersecurity. These federally sponsored exercises, known as Cyber Storm, provide the opportunity for sector participants to exercise strategic decision making and interagency coordination of incident responses, and to test information-sharing processes for collecting and disseminating cyber incident situational awareness across sectors. Each Cyber Storm builds on lessons learned to develop a more sophisticated and challenging incident scenario for the next exercise.

8.3 Implementing the Sector Partnership Model

Section 1.2 of this document discusses the various classes of entities and individuals who play a role in protecting the Critical Manufacturing Sector. This section describes the primary mechanisms DHS uses to coordinate with those CIKR partners through the NIPP sector partnership model.

8.3.1 Coordinating With Private Sector Owner/Operators and Organizations

The majority of the assets in the Critical Manufacturing Sector are privately owned and operated. Consequently, there must be a strong collaboration between DHS and the private sector to ensure both the efficient integration of industry programs with DHS Critical Manufacturing Sector protective programs and the overall effectiveness of the goals and initiatives laid out in this document. A true Federal/private sector partnership can only come about through routine engagement between DHS and the private sector. The principal means for developing and sustaining this partnership is the CMSCC.

The CMSCC includes manufacturing companies that are critical to the American economy, both domestically and internationally. The CMSCC's structure aligns with HSPD-7's goal of protecting the Nation from terrorist attacks and natural disasters that could "damage the private sector's capability to ensure the orderly functioning of the economy and delivery of essential services; have a negative effect on the economy through the cascading disruption of other critical infrastructure and key resources;

or undermine the public's morale and confidence in our national economic and political institutions." For this purpose, the CMSCC shall include private sector heavy manufacturing companies and manufacturing firms of any size that comprise U.S. critical infrastructure and/or provide key resources or that are considered iconic representatives of the U.S. economy. At a minimum, it will be representational of "critical manufacturing" industries as identified by DHS policy.

The Council will serve as the primary liaison between the Critical Manufacturing Sector and the United States Government at all levels concerning policy, strategy, and planning issues as outlined by the Council's mission. The SSA will coordinate with the CMSCC through regular meetings, conference calls, electronic mail, and other forms of communication to ensure close collaboration and partnership for all Critical Manufacturing Sector activities.

Current membership of the CMSCC includes representatives from the following companies:

- General Motors
- Chrysler Corporation
- John Deere
- Navistar
- U.S. Steel
- Ford Motor Company
- Boeing
- Bridgestone
- ArcelorMittal USA

- Kohler
- General Electric
- Schweitzer Engineering Laboratories, Inc.
- Carpenter Technology Corporation
- Emerson
- ITT Corporation
- Cisco Systems
- Intel Corporation
- Smith and Wesson

8.3.2 Coordination Among Government Entities

As part of the NIPP, the CMGCC serves as the formal entity for coordinating government-led sector CIKR protection activities. The CMGCC consists of representatives from a wide variety of government stakeholders in Critical Manufacturing whose engagement is necessary to efficiently and effectively enhance sector resilience and protection.

The Council will serve as a forum for communication between the Federal government (including the SSA), the CMSCC, and all other relevant sector partners concerning policy, strategy, and planning issues. The SSA will coordinate with the CMGCC through regular meetings, conference calls, electronic mail, and other forms of communication to ensure close collaboration and partnership for all Critical Manufacturing Sector activities.

Current membership of the CMGCC includes representatives from:

- Environmental Protection Agency
- Federal Bureau of Investigation
- Small Business Administration
- State, Local, Tribal, and Territorial GCC
- United States Department of Commerce
- United States Department of Defense
- United States Department of Energy

- United States Department of Homeland Security
- United States Department of Justice
- United States Department of Labor
- United States Department of State
- United States Department of Transportation
- United States Department of Treasury

8.4 Information Sharing and Protection

8.4.1 Information Sharing

Development and maintenance of Critical Manufacturing Sector public-private partnership requires routine information sharing among all sector partners. The number and diversity of Critical Manufacturing Sector partners throughout the Nation presents a significant challenge to DHS regarding communicating with all of them. Efforts will be made to communicate with all sector partners by utilizing Federal agencies, State and local authorities, and other resources to identify and reach out to the sector. Additionally, the SSA will continuously promote outreach and awareness of the Critical Manufacturing CIKR protection mission at relevant conferences and workshops.

8.4.1.1 Homeland Security Information Network—Critical Sectors

In order to facilitate information sharing within the law enforcement community, the Federal Government developed an information sharing tool known as the Joint Regional Information Exchange System. Over time, that program was brought under DHS supervision and was renamed the Homeland Security Information Network (HSIN). In light of the enthusiasm with which the law enforcement community received HSIN, DHS has extended HSIN into the CIKR sectors identified in HSPD-7 through a parallel effort known as HSIN-Critical Sectors (HSIN-CS).

Under HSIN-CS, DHS is working with the GCCs and SCCs for each CIKR sector to develop an online information-sharing tool specific to each sector. HSIN-CS is designed to enable communication within a given sector, between multiple sectors, and between a sector and governmental entities. HSIN-CS offers four major components to network participants:

- **Alerts Broadcasting/Narrowcasting from DHS**—a secure medium for DHS and sector leaders to transmit actionable alerts and warnings about threats to critical infrastructure to a vetted audience.

- **HSIN-CS Portal**—a capability of storing sensitive documents, including sophisticated imaging and maps. The portal also enables real-time analysis of data and reporting tasks. The portal will provide a knowledge base that enables planning and coordination within and across all CIKR sectors.

- **Collaboration Tools**—a peer-to-peer collaboration space for members to engage in real-time dialogue. Members can create their own private groups to discuss defined topics and collaborate on common documents.

- **HSIN-CS Infrastructure**—an underlying technology platform and network upon which additional infrastructure can be added.

Within HSIN-CS, a secure portal is being designed for the Critical Manufacturing Sector, called HSIN-Critical Manufacturing. Using Protected Critical Infrastructure Information (PCII) and other available information protection mechanisms, sensitive business or security-related information maintained on HSIN will be kept private to the maximum extent allowed by law.

Additionally, the Critical Manufacturing Sector will establish a Critical Manufacturing Information Sharing Working Group (ISWG). The ISWG will serve as a joint (CMSCC and CMGCC) working group that will address information-sharing issues of concern to the sector, including information-sharing policy and practices with regard to communication, collaboration and coordination, and operational awareness. Furthermore, the ISWG will articulate and explore the accommodation of information-sharing requirements for Critical Manufacturing CIKR protection and resilience business and mission activities.

8.4.1.2 Cybersecurity Information Sharing

The sector is an active participant in working groups established to raise awareness of cybersecurity issues across all CIKR sectors. Both the SSA and private sector partners attend meetings to stay apprised of the latest information and to provide sector input. Two important working groups are:

- **Cross-Sector Cyber Security Working Group (CSCSWG):** This working group provides a forum to bring government and private sector partners together to work collaboratively to address risk across all CIKR sectors under the CIPAC framework. The CSCSWG addresses a wide variety of cybersecurity issues and enables comprehensive planning and sharing of information across the community of interested stakeholders.

- **Industrial Control Systems Joint Working Group (ICSJWG):** This group is a collaborative effort among various stakeholders involved in industrial control systems, including participants from the international community, government, academia, vendors, owners and operators, and systems integrators. Stakeholders have the opportunity to address efforts of mutual interest, build upon existing efforts, reduce redundancies, and contribute to national and international security.

Additionally, information on cybersecurity is shared among sector partners primarily through the United States Computer Emergency Readiness Team (US-CERT). US-CERT, a public/private partnership established in 2003 to protect the Nation's Internet infrastructure, is responsible for coordinating defenses against and responses to cyber attacks across the Nation. As part of this responsibility, US-CERT (**www.us-cert.gov**) interacts with Federal agencies, industry, the research community, State and local governments, and others to disseminate reasoned and actionable cybersecurity information to the public.

8.4.1.3 Sharing of Threat Information

The DHS and other Federal partners share threat-related information with sector partners primarily through the Homeland Infrastructure Threat and Risk Analysis Center (HITRAC), described in greater detail in section 3.5.

8.4.2 Information Protection

Often, the information used by DHS and its CIKR partners to effectively manage risk and protect the Nation's critical infrastructure will contain sensitive security information and/or sensitive business and proprietary information. As a result, information protection is a significant concern for those CIKR partners who supply this sensitive information. The DHS takes the need to protect this information extremely seriously, and will do so to the maximum extent allowed by law.

8.4.2.1 Protected Critical Infrastructure Information (PCII)

Pursuant to the Critical Infrastructure Information Act (CIIA) of 2002, a critical infrastructure information program was created under which sensitive and proprietary critical infrastructure information submitted to DHS, if it satisfies the requirements of the CIIA, will be protected from public disclosure to the maximum extent permitted by law. The PCII Program is managed by the Infrastructure Information Collection Division within the Office of Infrastructure Protection. The rules governing the PCII Program are located in Title 6, Part 29 of the Code of Federal Regulations. General information on the PCII Program, including instructions on how to properly submit information in compliance with the program, can be found on the DHS web site at **www.dhs.gov/pcii**.

8.4.2.2 Critical Infrastructure Partnership Advisory Council (CIPAC)

The CIPAC is a partnership between government and private sector CIKR owners and operators to facilitate effective coordination of CIKR protection programs pursuant to section 121 of the Homeland Security Act and HSPD-7, across the full range of CIKR sectors. The private sector members of the CIPAC are the members of the various CIKR SCCs (including owners/operators, designated trade or equivalent organizations, and invited Subject Matter Experts), and the public sector members are DHS and the other members of the corresponding GCCs (including representatives from Federal, State, local, tribal, and territorial government entities). DHS has exercised its authority under section 871 of the Homeland Security Act to exempt the CIPAC from the Federal Advisory Committee Act (FACA). This ensures that the CIPAC members can discuss security-sensitive topics without the risk that these discussions could become public and jeopardize security. The CIPAC can meet as a whole, or in the form of joint committees specific to a particular sector.

Appendix 1: List of Acronyms and Abbreviations

BZP	Buffer Zone Plan
CII	Critical Infrastructure Information
CIIA	Critical Infrastructure Information Act
CIKR	Critical Infrastructure and Key Resources
CIP	Critical Infrastructure Protection
CIPAC	Critical Infrastructure Partnership Advisory Council
CMGCC	Critical Manufacturing Government Coordinating Council
CMSCC	Critical Manufacturing Sector Coordinating Council
DCS	Distributed Control Systems
DHS	Department of Homeland Security
FACA	Federal Advisory Committee Act
GCC	Government Coordinating Council
HITRAC	Homeland Infrastructure Threat and Risk Analysis Center
HSAC	Homeland Security Advisory Council
HSIN	Homeland Security Information Network
HSIN-CS	Homeland Security Information Network—Critical Sectors
HSPD	Homeland Security Presidential Directive
IDW	Infrastructure Data Warehouse
IP	Office of Infrastructure Protection
IPT	Integrated Product Team
NADB	National Asset Database
NAICS	North American Industry Classification System
NIAC	National Infrastructure Advisory Council
NIPP	National Infrastructure Protection Plan
OMB	Office of Management and Budget

PCII	Protected Critical Infrastructure Information
PCS	Process Control Systems
PVTSAC	Private Sector Senior Advisory Committee
R&D	Research and Development
RMA	Risk Mitigation Activities
S&T	Science and Technology Directorate
SAFETEA-LU Act	Safe, Accountable, Flexible, Efficient Transportation Equity Act: A Legacy for Users
SCADA	Supervisory Control and Data Acquisition
SCC	Sector Coordinating Council
SLTTGCC	State, Local, Tribal, and Territorial Government Coordinating Council
SSA	Sector-Specific Agency
SSA EMO	Sector-Specific Agency Executive Management Office
SSP	Sector-Specific Plan
US-CERT	United States Computer Emergency Readiness Team

Appendix 2: Glossary

Asset. Person, structure, facility, information, material, or process that has value. In the context of the NIPP, people are not considered assets.

CIKR Partner. Those Federal, State, regional, local, tribal, or territorial government entities; private sector owners and operators and representative organizations; academic and professional entities; and certain nonprofit and private volunteer organizations that share in the responsibility for protecting the Nation's CIKR.

Consequence. The effect of an event, incident, or occurrence. For the purposes of the NIPP, consequences are divided into four main categories: public health and safety, economic, psychological, and governance impacts.

Control Systems. Computer-based systems used within many infrastructures and industries to monitor and control sensitive processes and physical functions. These systems typically collect measurement and operational data from the field, process and display the information, and relay control commands to local or remote equipment or human-machine interfaces (operators). Examples of types of control systems include Supervisory Control and Data Acquisition (SCADA) systems, Process Control Systems (PCS), and Distributed Control Systems (DCS).

Critical Infrastructure. Systems and assets, whether physical or virtual, so vital that the incapacity or destruction of such may have a debilitating impact on the security, economy, public health or safety, environment, or any combination of these matters, across any Federal, State, regional, territorial, or local jurisdiction.

Critical Infrastructure Information (CII). Information that is not customarily in the public domain and is related to the security of critical infrastructure or protected systems. CII consists of records and information concerning any of the following:

- Actual, potential, or threatened interference with, attack on, compromise of, or incapacitation of critical infrastructure or protected systems by either physical or computer-based attack or other similar conduct (including the misuse of or unauthorized access to all types of communications and data transmission systems) that violates Federal, State, or local law; harms the interstate commerce of the United States; or threatens public health or safety.

- The ability of any critical infrastructure or protected system to resist such interference, compromise, or incapacitation, including any planned or past assessment, projection, or estimate of the vulnerability of critical infrastructure or a protected system, including security testing, risk evaluation thereto, risk management planning, or risk audit.

- Any planned or past operational problem or solution regarding critical infrastructure or protected systems, including repair, recovery, insurance, or continuity, to the extent that it is related to such interference, compromise, or incapacitation.

Cybersecurity. The prevention of damage to, unauthorized use of, or exploitation of, and, if needed, the restoration of electronic information and communication systems and the information contained therein to ensure confidentiality, integrity, and availability. Includes protection and restoration, when needed, of information networks and wireline, wireless, satellite, public safety answering points, and 911 communication systems and control systems.

Dependency. The one-directional reliance of an asset, system, network, or collection thereof, within or across sectors, on input, interaction, or other requirement from other sources in order to function properly.

Government Coordinating Council (GCC). The government counterpart to the Sector Coordinating Council (SCC) for each sector established to enable interagency coordination. The GCC is comprised of representatives across various levels of government (Federal, State, local, tribal, and territorial) as appropriate to the security and operational landscape of each individual sector.

Incident. An occurrence, caused by either human action or natural phenomena, that may cause harm and may require action. Incidents can include major disasters, emergencies, terrorist attacks, terrorist threats, wild and urban fires, floods, hazardous materials spills, nuclear accidents, aircraft accidents, earthquakes, hurricanes, tornadoes, tropical storms, war-related disasters, public health and medical emergencies, and other occurrences requiring an emergency response.

Infrastructure. The framework of interdependent networks and systems comprising identifiable industries, institutions (including people and procedures), and distribution capabilities that provide a reliable flow of products and services essential to the defense and economic security of the United States, the smooth functioning of government at all levels, and society as a whole. Consistent with the definition in the Homeland Security Act of 2002, infrastructures include physical, cyber, and/or human elements.

Interdependency. Mutually reliant relationship between entities (objects, individuals, or groups). The degree of interdependency does not need to be equal in both directions.

Key Resources. As defined in the Homeland Security Act, key resources are publicly or privately controlled resources essential to the minimal operation of the economy and government.

Mitigation. Ongoing and sustained action to reduce the probability of or lessen the impact of an adverse incident.

Network. A group of components that share information or interact with each other in order to perform a function.

Normalize. In the context of the NIPP, the process of transforming risk-related data into comparable units.

Owners and Operators. Those entities responsible for day-to-day operation and investment in a particular asset or system.

Preparedness. Activities necessary to build, sustain, and improve readiness capabilities to prevent, protect against, respond to, and recover from natural or manmade incidents. Preparedness is a continuous process involving efforts at all levels of government and between government and the private sector and nongovernmental organizations to identify threats, determine vulnerabilities, and identify required resources to prevent, respond to, and recover from major incidents.

Prevention. Actions taken and measures put in place for the continual assessment and readiness of necessary actions to reduce the risk of threats and vulnerabilities, to intervene and stop an occurrence, or to mitigate effects.

Prioritization. In the context of the NIPP, prioritization is the process of using risk assessment results to identify where risk-reduction or mitigation efforts are most needed and subsequently determine which protective actions should be instituted in order to have the greatest effect.

Protection. Actions or measures taken to cover or shield from exposure, injury, or destruction. In the context of the NIPP, protection includes actions to deter the threat, mitigate the vulnerabilities, or minimize the consequences associated with a terrorist attack or other incident. Protection can include a wide range of activities, such as hardening facilities, building resiliency and redundancy, incorporating hazard resistance into initial facility design, initiating active or passive countermeasures, installing security systems, promoting workforce surety, training and exercises, and implementing cybersecurity measures, among various others.

Recovery. The development, coordination, and execution of service- and site-restoration plans for affected communities and the reconstitution of government operations and services through individual, private sector, nongovernmental, and public assistance programs that identify needs and define resources; provide housing and promote restoration; address long-term care and treatment of affected persons; implement additional measures for community restoration; incorporate mitigation measures and techniques, as feasible; evaluate the incident to identify lessons learned; and develop initiatives to mitigate the effects of future incidents.

Response. Activities that address the short-term, direct effects of an incident, including immediate actions to save lives, protect property, and meet basic human needs. Response also includes the execution of emergency operations plans and incident mitigation activities designed to limit the loss of life, personal injury, property damage, and other unfavorable outcomes. As indicated by the situation, response activities include applying intelligence and other information to lessen the effects or consequences of an incident; increasing security operations; continuing investigations into the nature and source of the threat; ongoing surveillance and testing processes; providing immunizations, isolation, or quarantine; and conducting specific law enforcement operations aimed at preempting, interdicting, or disrupting illegal activity and apprehending actual perpetrators and bringing them to justice.

Risk. The potential for an unwanted outcome resulting from an incident, event, or occurrence, as determined by its likelihood and the associated consequences.

Risk Management Framework. A planning methodology that outlines the process for setting goals and objectives; identifying assets, systems, and networks; assessing risks; prioritizing and implementing protection programs and resiliency strategies; measuring performance; and taking corrective action. Public and private sector entities often include risk management frameworks in their business continuity plans.

Sector. A logical collection of assets, systems, networks, or functions that provide a common function to the economy, government, or society. The NIPP addresses 18 CIKR sectors, as identified by the criteria set forth in HSPD-7.

Sector Coordinating Council (SCC). The private sector counterpart to the GCCs, these councils are self-organized, self-run, and self-governed organizations that are representative of a spectrum of key stakeholders within a sector. SCCs serve as the government's principal point of entry into each sector for developing and coordinating a wide range of CIKR protection activities and issues.

Sector Partnership Model. The framework used to promote and facilitate sector and cross-sector planning, coordination, collaboration, and information sharing for CIKR protection involving all levels of government and private sector entities.

Sector-Specific Agency (SSA). Federal departments and agencies identified in HSPD-7 as responsible for coordinating CIKR protection activities in specified CIKR sectors.

Sector-Specific Plan (SSP). Augmenting plans that complement and extend the NIPP Base Plan and detail the application of the NIPP framework specific to each CIKR sector. SSPs are developed by the SSAs in close collaboration with other sector partners.

System. Any combination of facilities, equipment, personnel, procedures, and communications integrated for a specific purpose.

Terrorism. Premeditated threat or act of violence against noncombatant persons, property, and environmental or economic targets to induce fear, intimidate, coerce, or affect a government, the civilian population, or any segment thereof, in furtherance of political, social, ideological, or religious objectives.

Threat. A natural or manmade occurrence, individual, entity, or action that has or indicates the potential to harm life, information, operations, the environment, and/or property.

Value Proposition. A statement that outlines the national and homeland security interest in protecting the Nation's CIKR and articulates benefits gained by all partners through the risk management framework and public-private partnership described in the NIPP.

Vulnerability. A physical feature or operational attribute that renders an entity open to exploitation or susceptible to a given hazard.

Appendix 3: Authorities

Owners and operators of assets in the Critical Manufacturing Sector are subject to a wide variety of existing authorities and regulations. This appendix sets forth those regulations that are helping to protect the Critical Manufacturing Sector.[4]

The paragraphs below outline the authorities vested in different Federal agencies that relate to CIKR protection in the Critical Manufacturing Sector, either directly or indirectly, and which provide essential support to DHS in securing the Critical Manufacturing Sector. Additionally, many of the rules and regulations below apply to chemicals or other hazardous materials that may not apply in all functional areas of the Critical Manufacturing Sector.

Homeland Security Act of 2002 (Public Law 107-296): Establishes a Cabinet-level department headed by a Secretary of Homeland Security with the mandate and legal authority to protect the American people from the continuing threat of terrorism. DHS's mission is to prevent terrorist attacks within the United States; reduce the vulnerability of the United States to terrorism at home; minimize the damage and assist in the recovery from terrorist attacks that occur; and ensure that the overall economic security of the United States is not diminished by efforts, activities, and programs aimed at securing the homeland. To fulfill another mission, protection of CIKR, the DHS is to complete comprehensive assessments of CIKR vulnerabilities, including the performance of risk assessments to determine the risks posed by particular types of terrorist attacks; develop a comprehensive national plan for securing CIKR and the physical and technological assets that support such systems; and recommend measures necessary to protect CIKR in coordination with other agencies of the Federal Government and in cooperation with State and local government agencies and authorities, the private sector, and other entities. Those requirements, combined with the President's direction in the HSPD-7, mandate the unified approach to CIKR protection taken in the NIPP.

Homeland Security Presidential Directive 7 (HSPD-7): HSPD-7 established a national policy and framework for Federal departments and agencies to identify, prioritize, and protect CIKR from terrorist attacks, with an emphasis on protecting against catastrophic health effects and mass casualties. It mandates creation and implementation of the NIPP and sets forth roles and responsibilities for the DHS; SSAs; other Federal departments and agencies; and State, local, tribal, private sector, and other sector partners.

Homeland Security Presidential Directive 5 (HSPD-5): HSPD-5 establishes a national approach to domestic incident management that ensures effective coordination among all levels of government, and between the government and the private sector. Central to this approach is the National Incident Management System (NIMS), an organizational framework for all levels of government, and the National Response Framework (NRF), an operational framework for national incident response.

Homeland Security Presidential Directive 8 (HSPD-8): HSPD-8 establishes policies to strengthen the preparedness of the United States to prevent, protect, respond to, and recover from threatened or actual domestic terrorist attacks, major disasters,

---

[4] Note, this appendix is not meant to be a comprehensive list of all regulations impacting the Critical Manufacturing Sector, but instead simply seeks to identify some of the major regulations along with the corresponding agencies responsible for implementing them.

and other emergencies by requiring a national domestic all-hazards preparedness goal; establishing mechanisms for improved delivery of Federal preparedness assistance to State and local governments; and outlining actions to strengthen the preparedness capabilities of Federal, State, and local entities. This directive mandates the development of the goal to guide emergency preparedness training, planning, equipment, and exercises, and to ensure that all entities involved adhere to the same standards. The directive calls for an inventory of Federal response capabilities and refines the process by which preparedness grants are administered, disbursed, and utilized at the State and local levels.

Chemical Facility Anti-Terrorism Standards (CFATS): In Section 550 of the Department of Homeland Security Appropriations Act of 2007, Congress gave DHS the authority to require high-risk chemical facilities to complete vulnerability assessments, develop site security plans, and implement protective measures necessary to meet DHS-defined performance standards. In accordance with this authority, on April 2, 2007, DHS released the Chemical Facility Anti-Terrorism Standards as an interim final rule. While CFATS focuses on chemical facilities, many facilities within the Critical Manufacturing Sector also fall under the regulations due to the storage and use of chemicals.

Through the CFATS, DHS established risk-based performance standards for the security of the Nation's chemical facilities. The CFATS require covered chemical facilities to prepare Security Vulnerability Assessments (SVA), which identify facility security vulnerabilities, and to develop and implement Site Security Plans, which include measures that satisfy the identified risk-based performance standards. It also allows certain covered chemical facilities, in specified circumstances, to submit Alternate Security Programs (ASPs) in lieu of an SVA, Site Security Plan, or both.

The CFATS also contain associated provisions addressing inspections and audits, recordkeeping, and the protection of information that constitutes Chemical-terrorism Vulnerability Information (CVI). Finally, the rule provides the Department with authority to seek compliance through the issuance of Orders, including Orders Assessing Civil Penalty and Orders for the Cessation of Operations.

Additional details on the CFATS interim final rule can be found by accessing the DHS website at **www.dhs.gov/chemicalsecurity**.

Maritime Transportation Security Act (MTSA): Under the MTSA (46 U.S.C. 70101 et seq.), the U.S. Coast Guard (USCG) has authority over the transportation of goods via water, as well as authority over the security of facilities adjacent to navigable waters that may be involved in transportation security incidents. This authority includes the collection and maintenance of essential infrastructure information concerning these facilities and review and approval of facility security assessments (FSAs) and facility security plans (FSPs).

Under the MTSA, the USCG is to establish area maritime security committees and prepare area maritime security plans for maritime security (33 CFR 102 and 103), which require assessments of ports, vessels, and U.S. facilities to identify those that pose a high risk of being involved in a transportation security incident. Additionally, the MTSA requires owners and operators of facilities located contiguous to waterways to complete FSAs and submit FSPs to the USCG for review and approval (33 CFR 105). FSPs must include security measures; procedures for responding to security threats; and detailed preparedness, prevention, and response activities for each marine security (MARSEC) level. High-risk vessels must also submit security assessments and security plans (33 CFR 104). The USCG also ensures that foreign flag vessels meet certain security standards (33 CFR 104.105(c)).

Clean Air Act: Under section 112(r) of the Clean Air Act (42 U.S.C. 7401-7671q), any facility that stores, processes, uses, or otherwise handles certain regulated substances above specific threshold amounts is required to develop and submit to the EPA a Risk Management Plan (RMP). The RMP must provide information on the regulated substances handled at the facility, an assessment of worst-case release scenario(s) and alternative release scenario(s), a five-year accident history of the facility, and information about the chemical accident prevention and emergency response programs at the facility.

Emergency Planning and Community Right-to-Know Act (EPCRA): Under EPCRA (42 U.S.C. 11001-11050), States are required to establish State emergency response commissions (SERCs), which, in turn, are required to establish local emergency planning committees (LEPCs). LEPCs are to develop local emergency response plans for releases of extremely hazardous substances (EHS). Each facility that handles EHS in excess of threshold quantities must notify the LEPC and must report any releases over a threshold quantity to the LEPC. If the facility is required under the Occupational Safety and Health Act of 1970 (29 U.S.C. 651 et seq.) to maintain material safety data sheets (MSDSs), the facility must submit an MSDS for each EHS onsite above the threshold quantity or a list of such substances, grouped by hazard (e.g., flammable, toxic), to the LEPC, the SERC, and the local fire department. The facilities must also submit annual inventories of hazardous materials managed at the facility over the threshold quantity during the previous year. The information submitted to the LEPC, the SERC, and the local fire department would be useful to DHS to identify at-risk facilities and to determine the mitigation measures and response measures necessary for and in place at each facility.

Superfund Amendments and Reauthorization Act of 1986: The passage of the Superfund Amendments and Reauthorization Act tasked the Centers for Disease Control and Prevention (CDC) Agency for Toxic Substances and Disease Registry with the responsibility for environmental public health logistical support in the event of a chemical release. This act broadened CDC's responsibilities in the areas of public health assessments, establishment and maintenance of toxicological databases, information dissemination, and medical education.

Occupational Safety and Health Act: The Occupational Safety and Health Act sets forth a variety of regulatory requirements placed upon employers to assure safe and healthful working conditions for working men and women by authorizing enforcement of the standards developed under the Act; assisting and encouraging the States in their efforts to assure safe and healthful working conditions; providing for research, information, education, and training in the field of occupational safety and health; and for other purposes.

Federal Explosives Laws (18 U.S.C. Chapter 40): Under the Federal explosives laws, the Bureau of Alcohol, Tobacco, Firearms, and Explosives (ATF) licenses manufacturers, dealers, and importers of explosives, and issues permits for users of explosives. Manufacturers, as well as other licensees and permittees, must submit to ATF the names and identifying information of responsible persons and employees, who must undergo criminal history background checks. Convicted felons, aliens, and other prohibited persons are disqualified from serving as responsible persons in the business or possessing explosives. Federal explosives law also requires all persons, including manufacturers, to comply with the Federal explosives storage requirements setting forth the standards of public safety and security to protect against explosives thefts, accidental explosions, and other safety and security hazards. For example, the magazines must meet certain construction requirements, bullet-proof standards, and table of distances specifications (e.g., explosive materials must be located a safe distance from public highways and inhabited dwellings). Additionally, manufacturers and other regulated entities must submit to ATF onsite inspections, maintain records of all explosives transactions, and report all thefts and losses of explosives. They must submit product samples upon request by ATF.

Defense Production Act of 1950 (DPA): Under Title I of the DPA, as amended (50 U.S.C. App. 2061 et seq.), the President is authorized to require preferential acceptance and performance of contracts or orders supporting certain approved national defense and energy programs, and to allocate materials, services, and facilities in such a manner as to promote these approved programs. The DPA authority has been extended to support emergency preparedness activities under Title VI of the Robert T. Stafford Disaster Relief and Emergency Assistance Act (the Stafford Act), as amended (42 U.S.C. 5195 et seq.). The DPA's definition of "national defense" was also amended in the December 2003 reauthorization of the Defense Production Act (Public Law 108-195) to include critical infrastructure protection and restoration. The President delegated the priorities and allocations authorities of the DPA in Executive Order 12919 (June 3, 1994; amended by Executive Order 13286, February 28, 2003). As part of that delegation, the President designated the Secretary of Commerce to administer the Defense Priorities and Allocations System (DPAS) (15 CFR 700). The Secretary of Commerce has delegated authority to the Secretaries of Defense, Energy, and Homeland Security, and to the Administrator of General Services to place, in accordance with the DPAS regulation, priority ratings on contracts or orders necessary or appropriate to promote the national defense. DHS may also endorse and forward to the Department of Commerce for appropriate action, the requests of owners or operators of critical infrastructure to place, in accordance with the DPAS regulation, priority ratings on contracts or orders in support of critical infrastructure protection or restoration-related programs determined by DHS as necessary or appropriate to promote the national defense.

Hazardous Materials Transportation Act: Under the Hazardous Materials Transportation Act (49 U.S.C. 5101 et seq., (HMTA)), DOT has the authority to promulgate regulations regarding the safe and secure shipment of hazardous materials (hazmat). Within DOT, this responsibility has been delegated to the Pipeline and Hazardous Materials Safety Administration (PHMSA) with enforcement authority shared by the modal administrations. Pursuant to this authority, PHMSA has established regulations governing the transportation of hazmat on public highways, by rail, in aircraft, and in vessels. In general, commercial hazmat move by permission of DOT granted through compliance with PHMSA's regulations, which are internationally harmonized to ensure that transportation is not unduly impeded. These regulations cover classification, packaging, emergency communication, training, and modal-specific requirements. Among PHMSA's rules are those that require offerors and transporters of certain types of hazmat to develop and implement security plans and conduct security training for employees. Security plans must be based on vulnerability assessments and must address personnel, access, and en route security related to hazmat in transportation. PHMSA ensures that the Nation's hazmat transportation rules are uniform through its preemptive authority over non-Federal requirements. PHMSA serves as the U.S. authority for hazmat transportation safety and security in international forums.

The Federal Motor Carrier Safety Administration (FMCSA) has also been delegated several authorities under the Hazardous Materials Transportation Act. These include the operational aspects of the vehicles used to carry the hazardous materials. In addition to routing and safety permits, FMCSA rules prohibit States from issuing, renewing, transferring, or upgrading a commercial driver's license with a hazmat endorsement, unless the TSA has first conducted a fingerprint-based records assessment of the applicant and determined that the applicant does not pose a security risk warranting denial of the hazmat endorsement (49 CFR Parts 383 and 384). The FMCSA also requires States to establish a hazmat endorsement renewal period of at least five years to ensure that each holder of a hazmat endorsement routinely and uniformly receives a security screening.

The HMTA was amended by the USA PATRIOT Act, Public Law 107-56, 115 Stat. 272, Section 1012, and, more recently, the SAFETEA-LU Act, Public Law 109-59 at 49 U.S.C. 5103a to require TSA, in conjunction with DOT, to administer safeguards for licensing hazardous material (hazmat) transport drivers. Pursuant to this responsibility, TSA published regulations that can be found at 49 CFR Part 1572. Under these rules, the roughly 3.5 million commercial drivers with hazmat endorsements on their commercial driver's licenses are required to undergo a periodic security assessment based on a review of FBI criminal records, and immigration and other relevant international databases, as appropriate.

Pipeline Safety Act: Through its authority under the Pipeline Safety Act (49 U.S.C. 60101 et seq.), PHMSA is responsible for ensuring the safe, reliable, and environmentally sound operation of the Nation's pipeline transportation system. PHMSA has safety jurisdiction over approximately 1.6 million miles of gas pipelines and an estimated 155,000 miles of hazardous liquid pipelines. Collaboration between PHMSA and DHS on the use of information concerning pipelines entering and leaving manufacturing facilities is essential to the responsibilities of both agencies.

Motor Carrier Safety Act of 1984: The Motor Carrier Safety Act prohibits the Secretary of Transportation from eliminating or modifying existing motor carrier safety rules pertaining to vehicles transporting hazardous substances unless and until an equivalent or more stringent regulation has been promulgated under the Hazardous Materials Transportation Act. Under this Act, FMCSA has issued rules related to parking and attendance of vehicles transporting hazardous materials.

Federal Rail Safety Act: Under authority designated from the Secretary of Transportation, the Federal Railroad Administration's regulatory responsibilities include the safe (and secure) movement of freight on railways across the United States. This responsibility includes the design, manufacture, and repair of the equipment, freight cars, locomotives, and track used to carry packaged hazmat, and the gathering of data on the movement of these chemicals throughout the United States, as well as internationally between the United States and Canada and Mexico.

Aviation Transportation and Security Act (ATSA) and DHS Delegation Number 7060.2: Under the ATSA (Public Law 107-71, 115 Stat. 597), and authority delegated under the Homeland Security Act, Section 403(2), and DHS Delegation Number 7060.2, TSA is responsible for the security of the movement of chemicals in all modes of transportation (49 U.S.C. 114(d)).

Trade Act of 2002: Section 343(a) of the Trade Act (Public Law 107-210, 116 Stat. 933), as amended by section 108 of the MTSA, requires DHS, through U.S. Customs and Border Protection (CBP) to collect electronic cargo information from all modes of commercial transport prior to the arrival of the cargo in, or its departure from, the United States. The information required must be sufficient to enable CBP to identify high-risk shipments. The regulations enforcing this requirement, 19 CFR Parts 4, 103, 113, 122, 123, 178, and 192, require advance transmission of electronic cargo information to CBP, by way of a CBP-approved electronic data interchange system. Such information must include the actual chemical name (not brand name) or the United Nations Hazmat code identifier number for all shipments of chemicals and hazardous materials. This information assists DHS in tracking the movement of hazardous materials in order to ensure cargo safety and security.